AF321576

After Empire

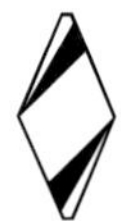

ISBN 978 94 9069 394 7 · D/2013/7852/158
published by AraMER an imprint of MER.
Paper Kunsthalle · merpaperkunsthalle.org
printed at New Goff **on** Arctic Volume Ivory
set in Arnhem & Frutiger

AFTER EMPIRE

Herman Asselberghs & Dieter Lesage

AFTER EMPIRE suggests an alternative for the iconic image that collective memory has kept as the quintessential moment of recent history: the hijacked plane hitting the second tower. For artist Herman Asselberghs and philosopher Dieter Lesage, this alternative to 9/11 would be: February 15, 2003. On that day, 30 million citizens across the planet marched against the unilateral decision by the American government to start a preemptive war against Iraq under the auspices of "the war on terror". It was the greatest peace demonstration since the Vietnam war, registered as the largest protest march ever. The war did happen, but this world day of dissent could very well mark the beginning of an empowering history of the 21st century: 2/15 instead of 9/11.

Nous partageons la même histoire
et c'est par là que tout commence.

Louis Althusser

BACK

CHAPTER I

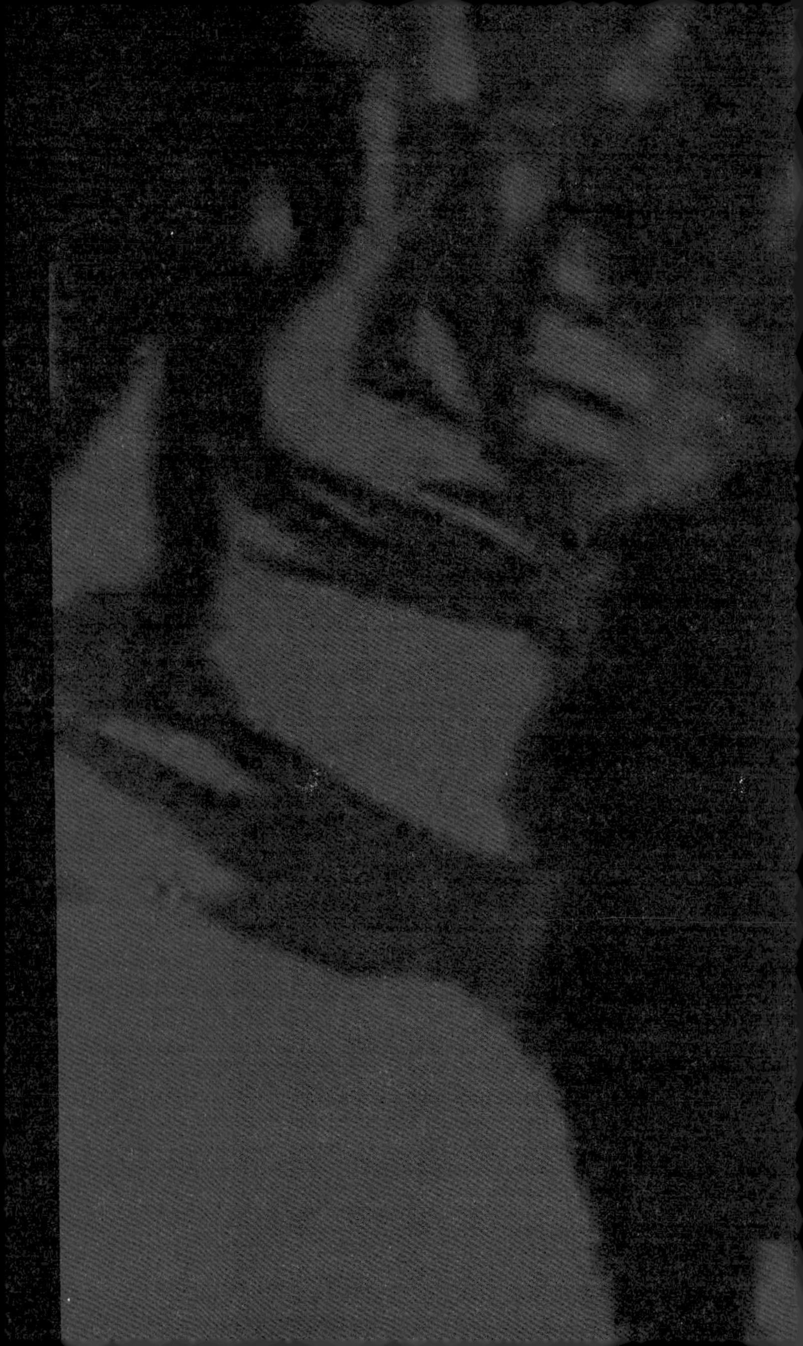

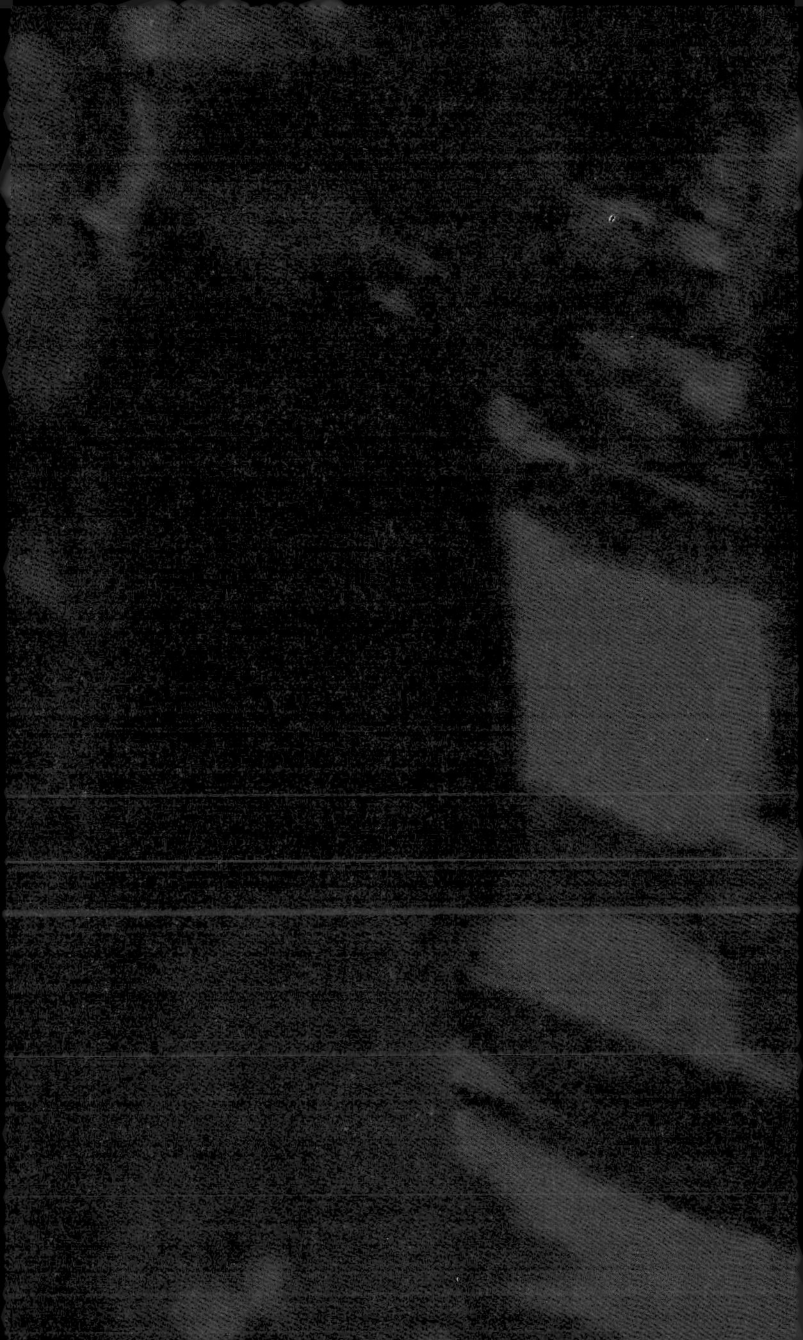

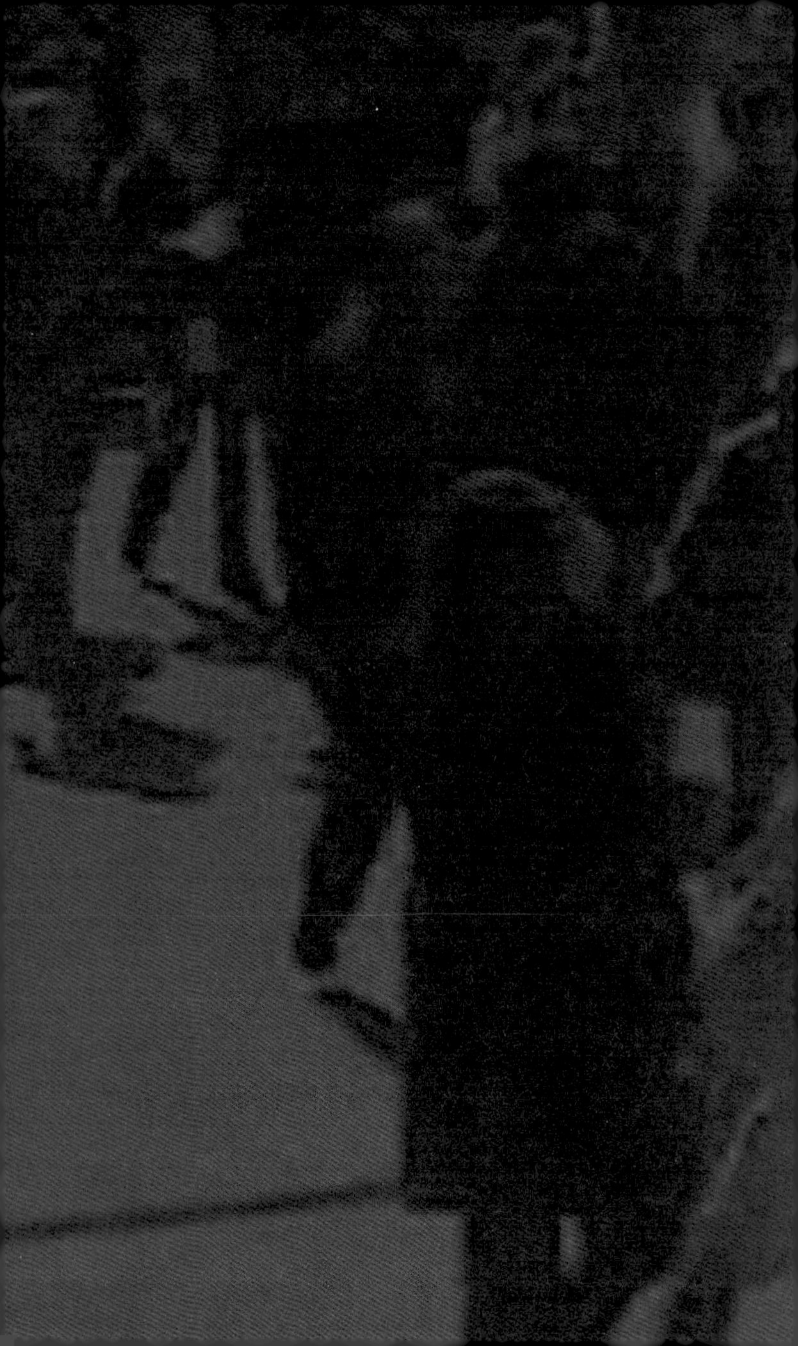

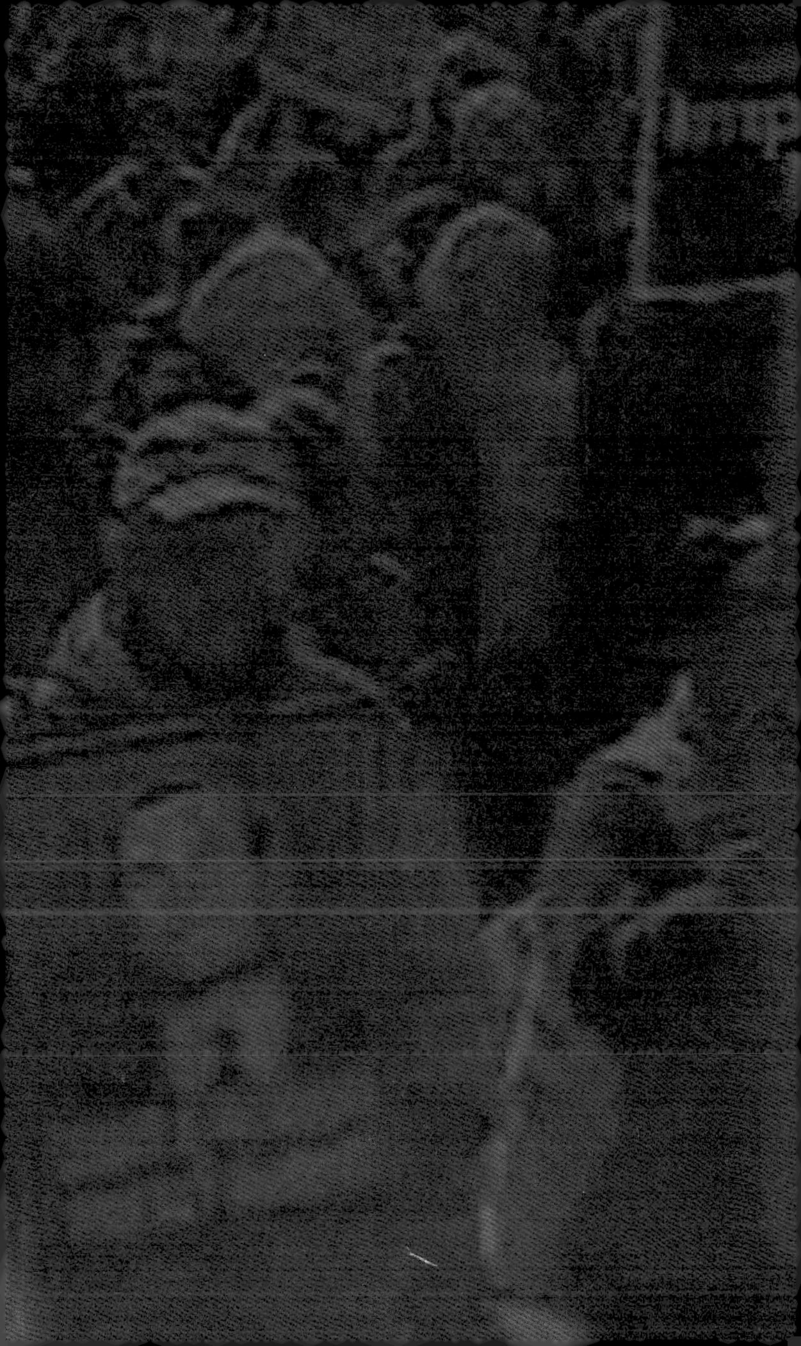

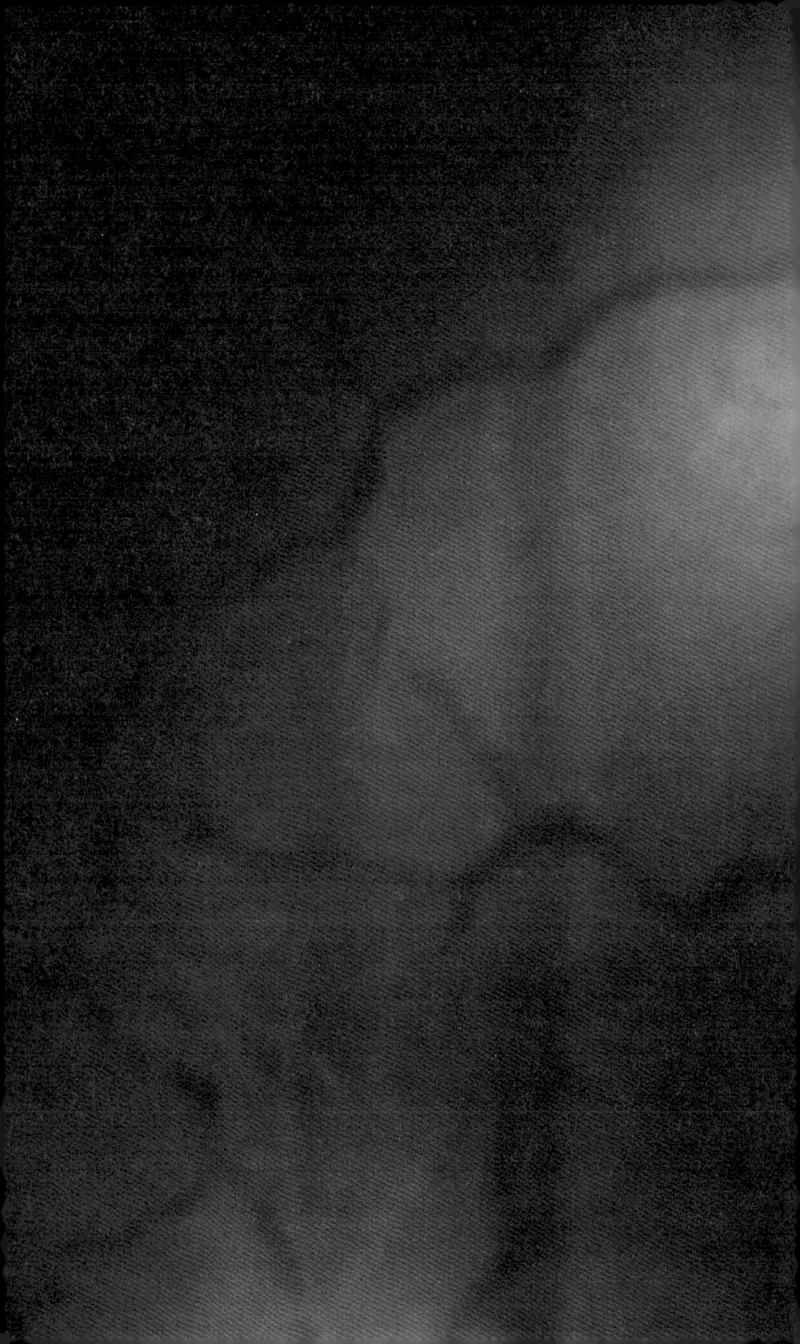

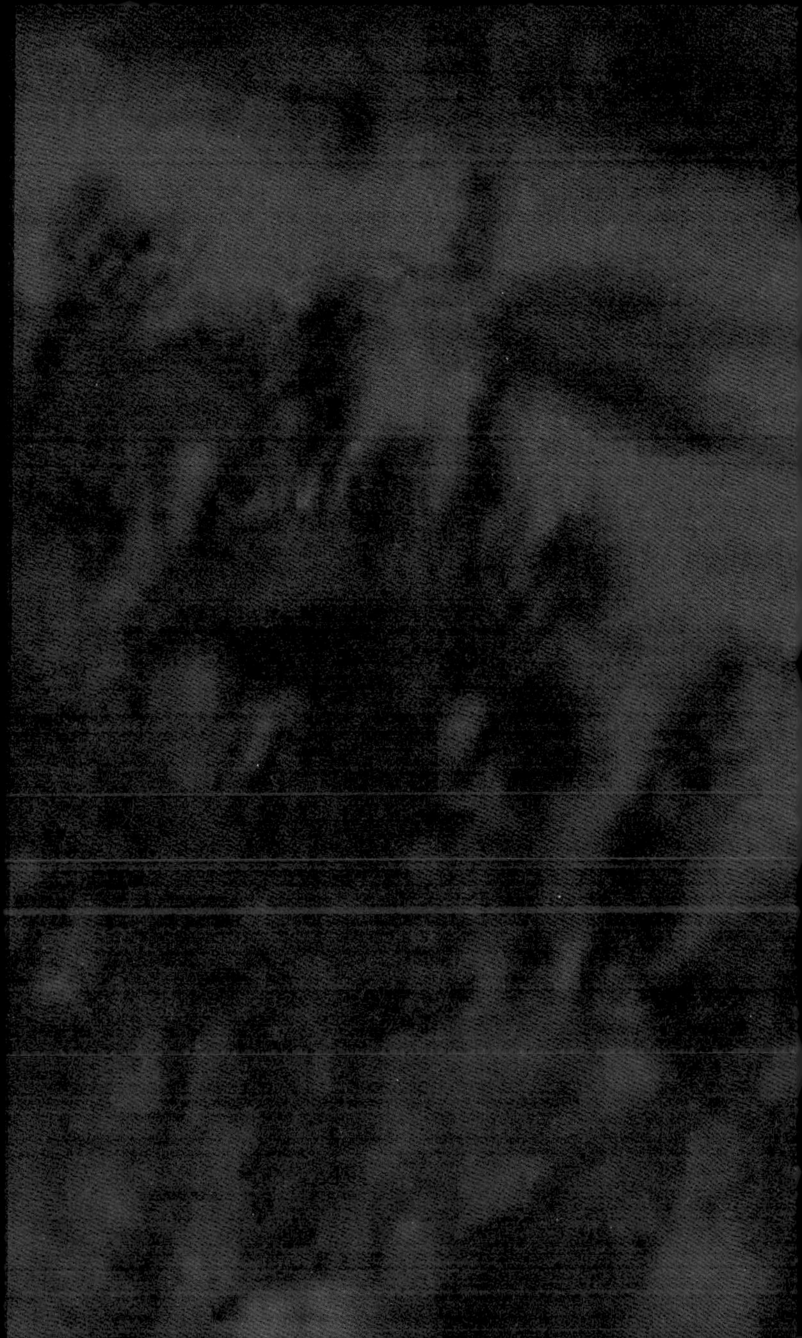

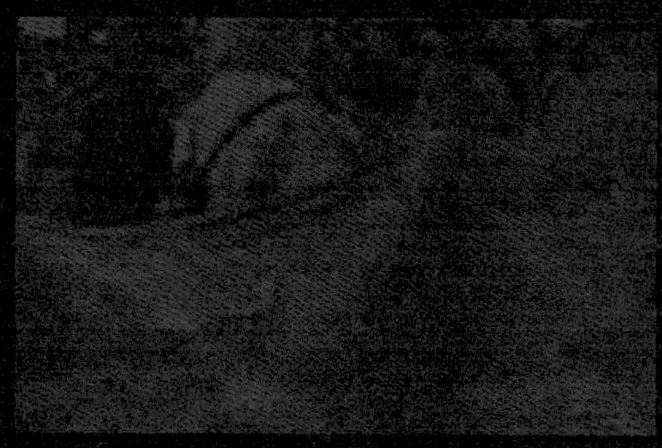

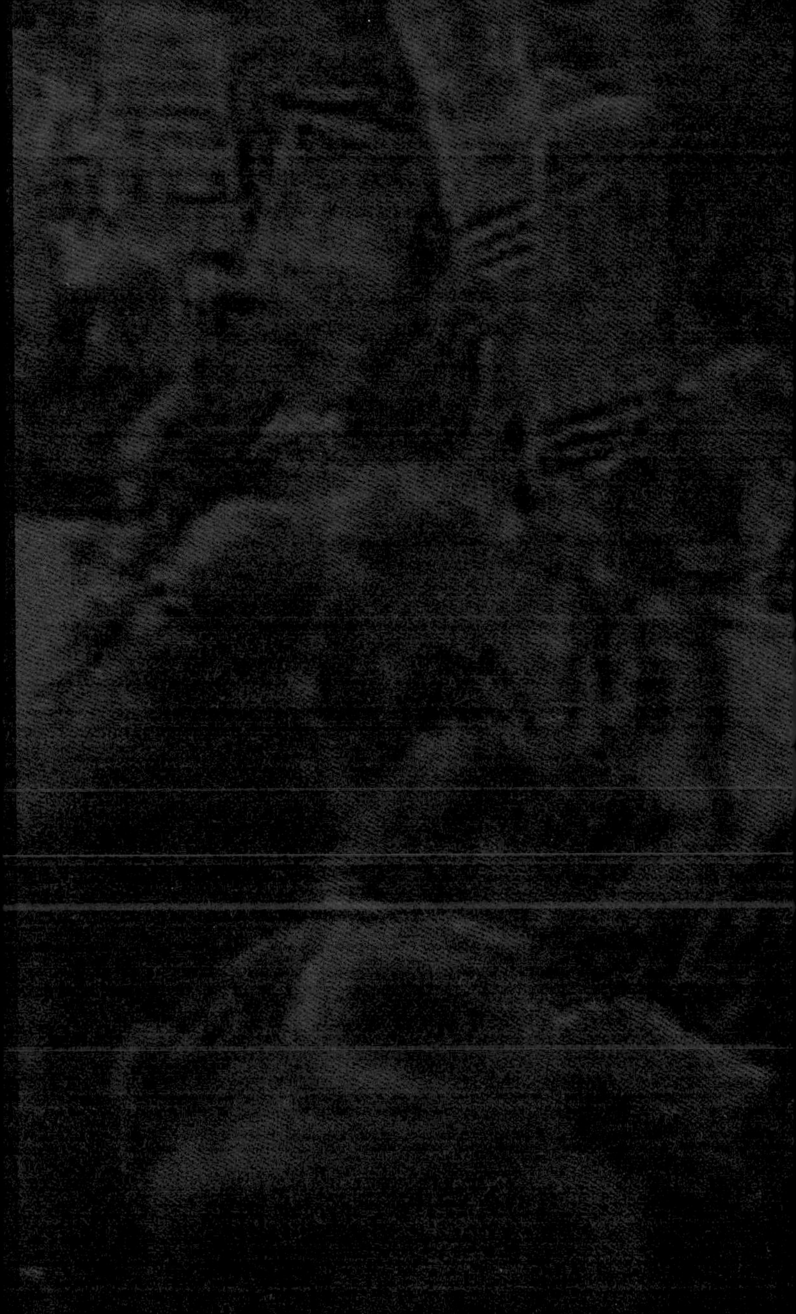

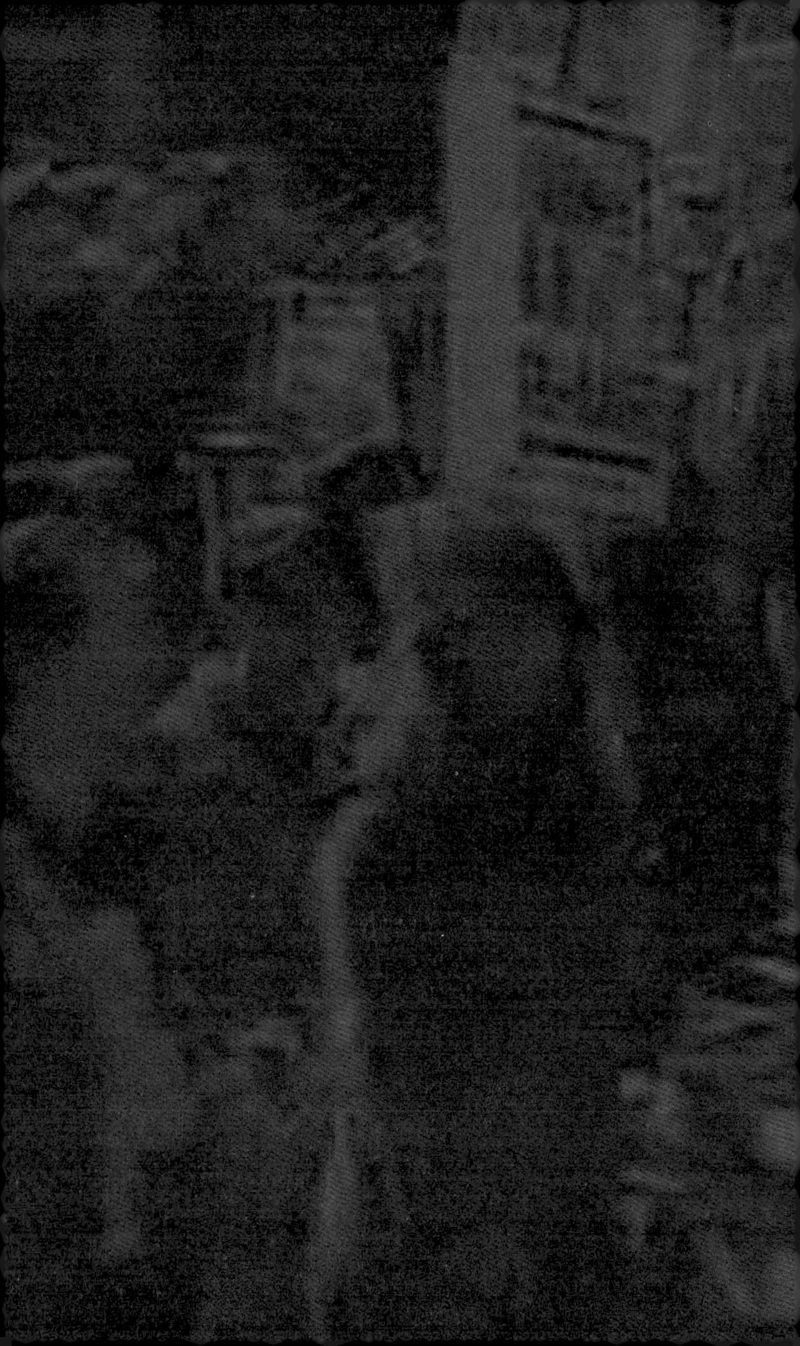

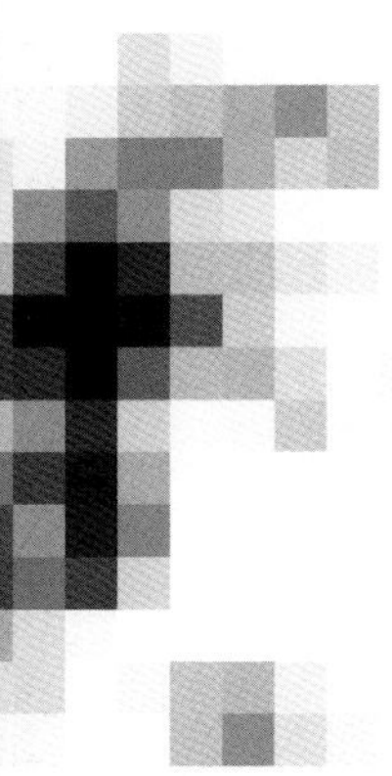

THIS

CHAPTER III

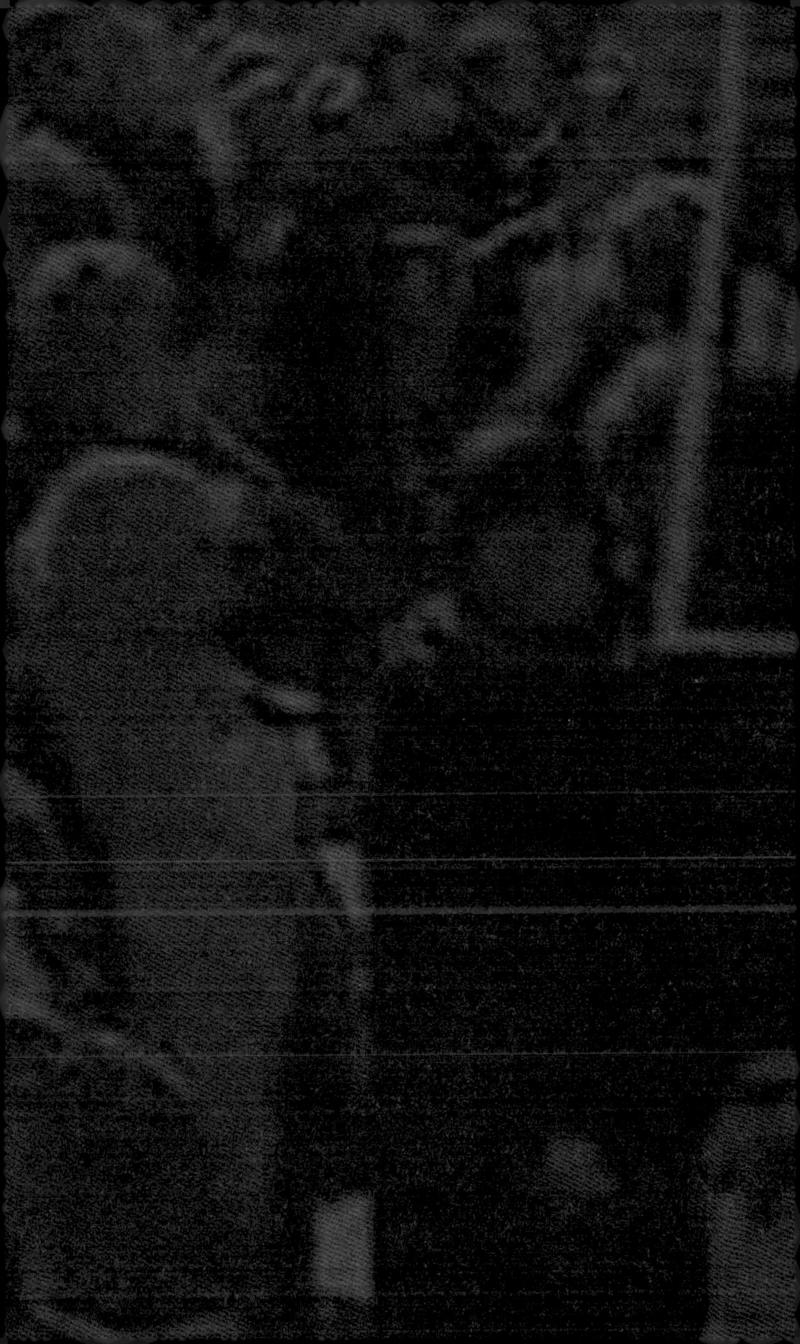

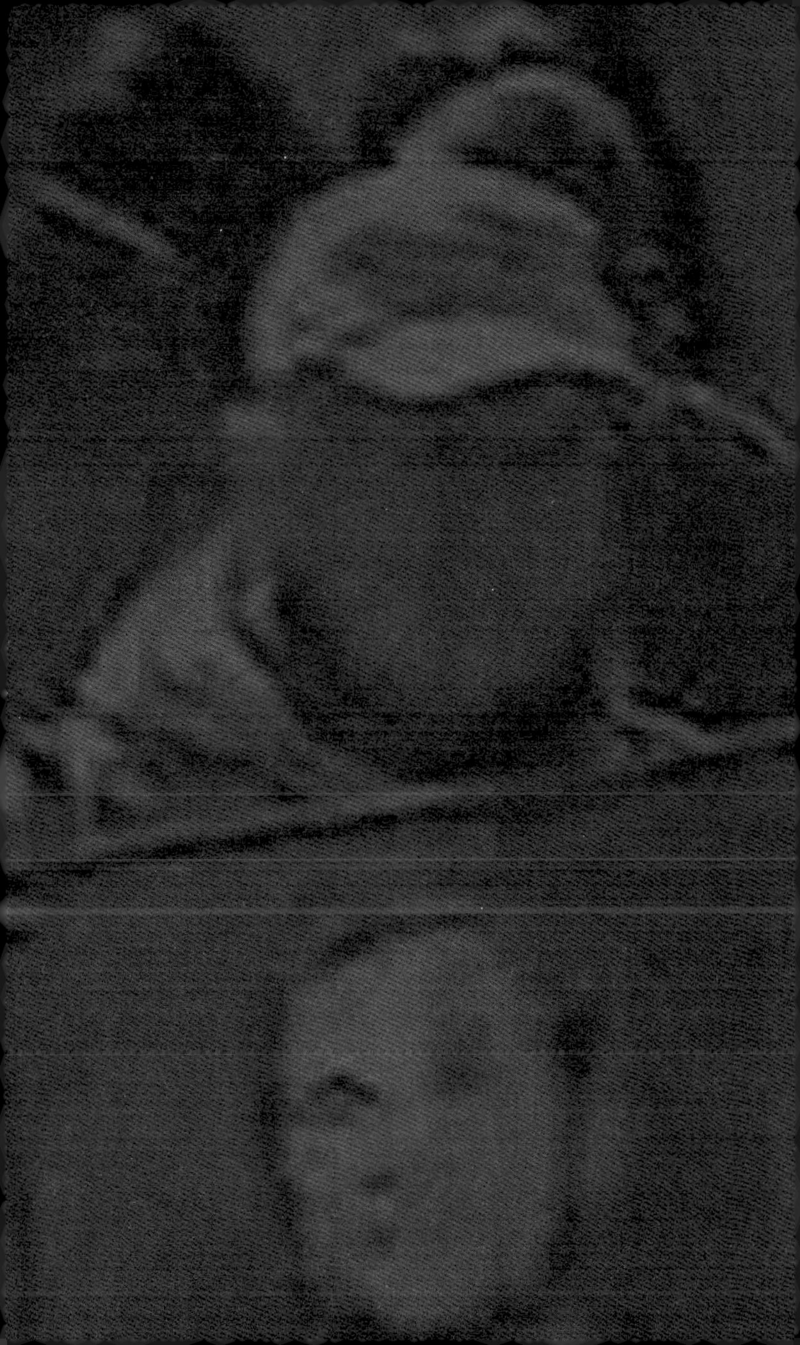

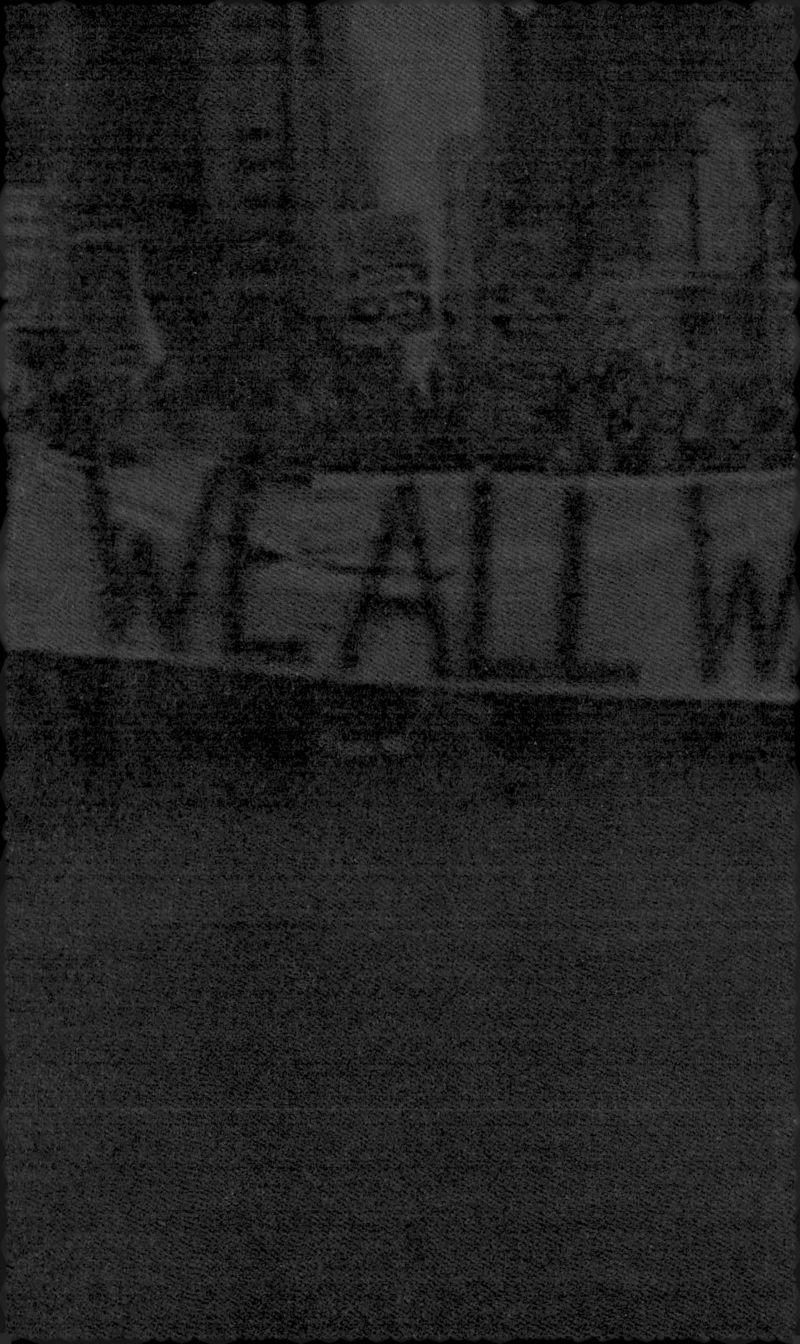

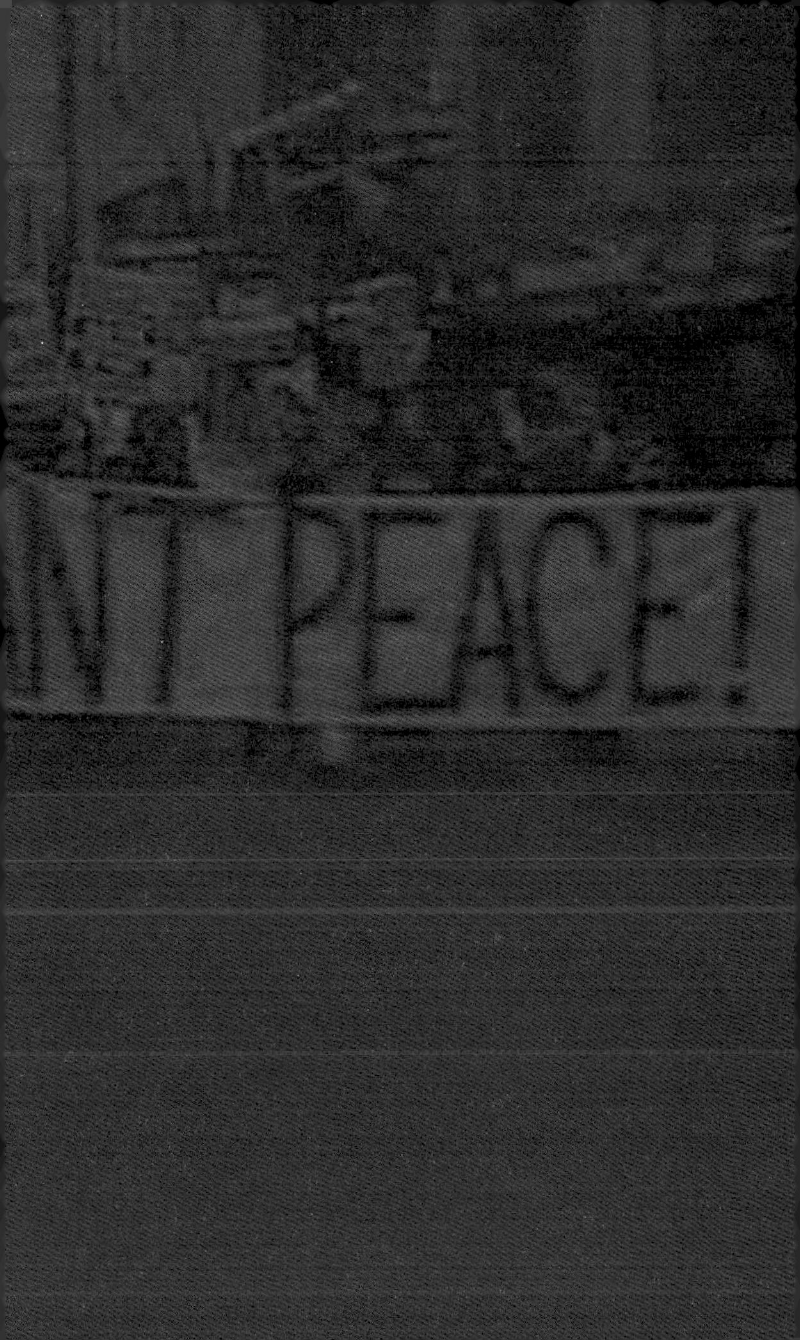
PEACE!

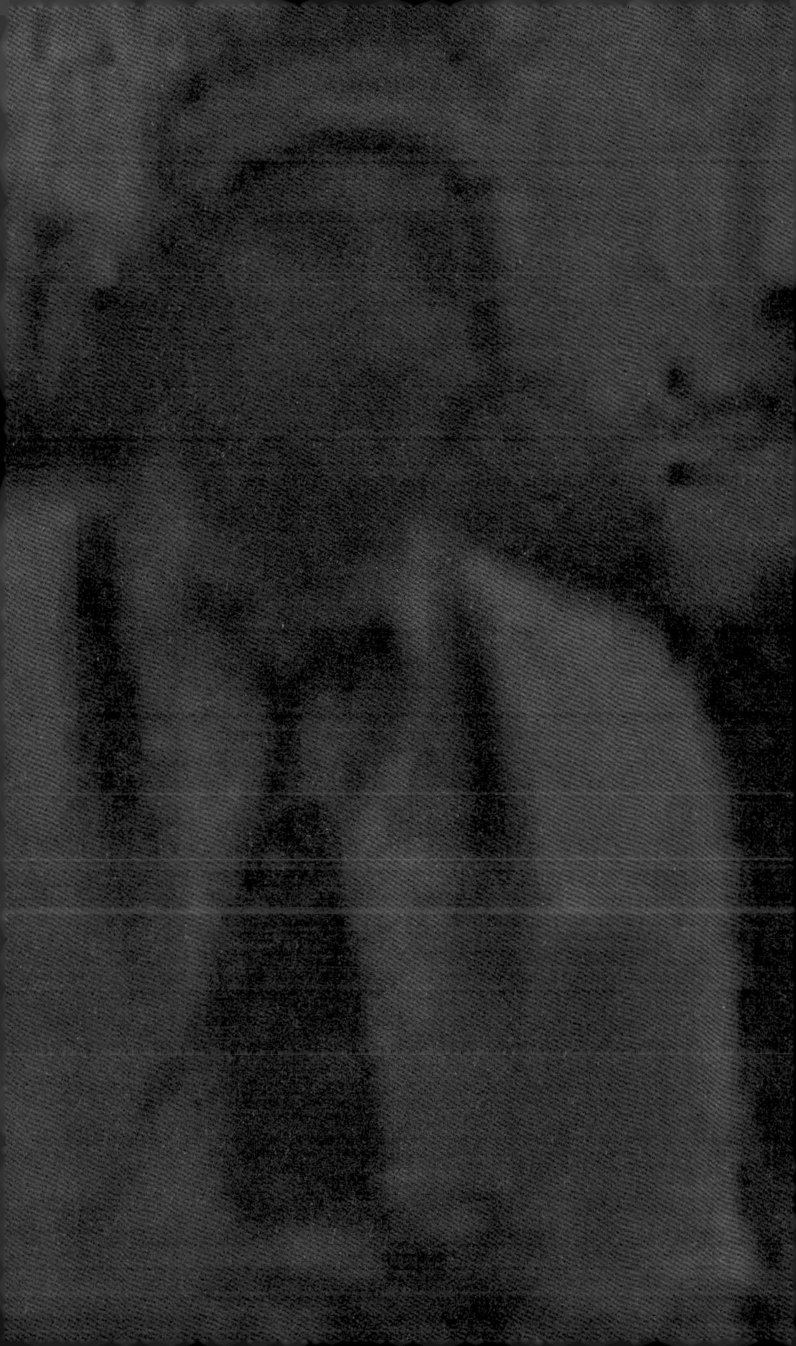

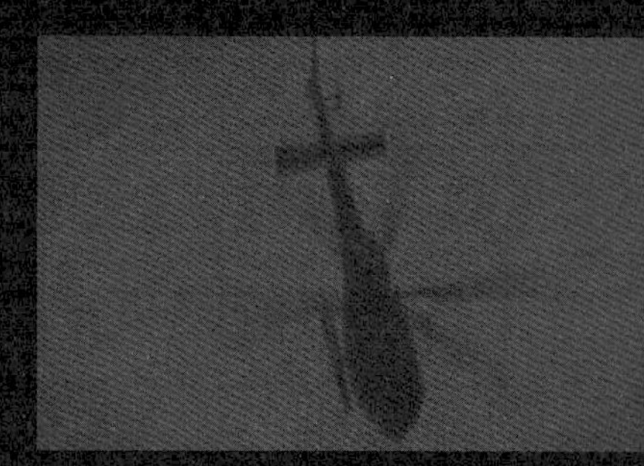

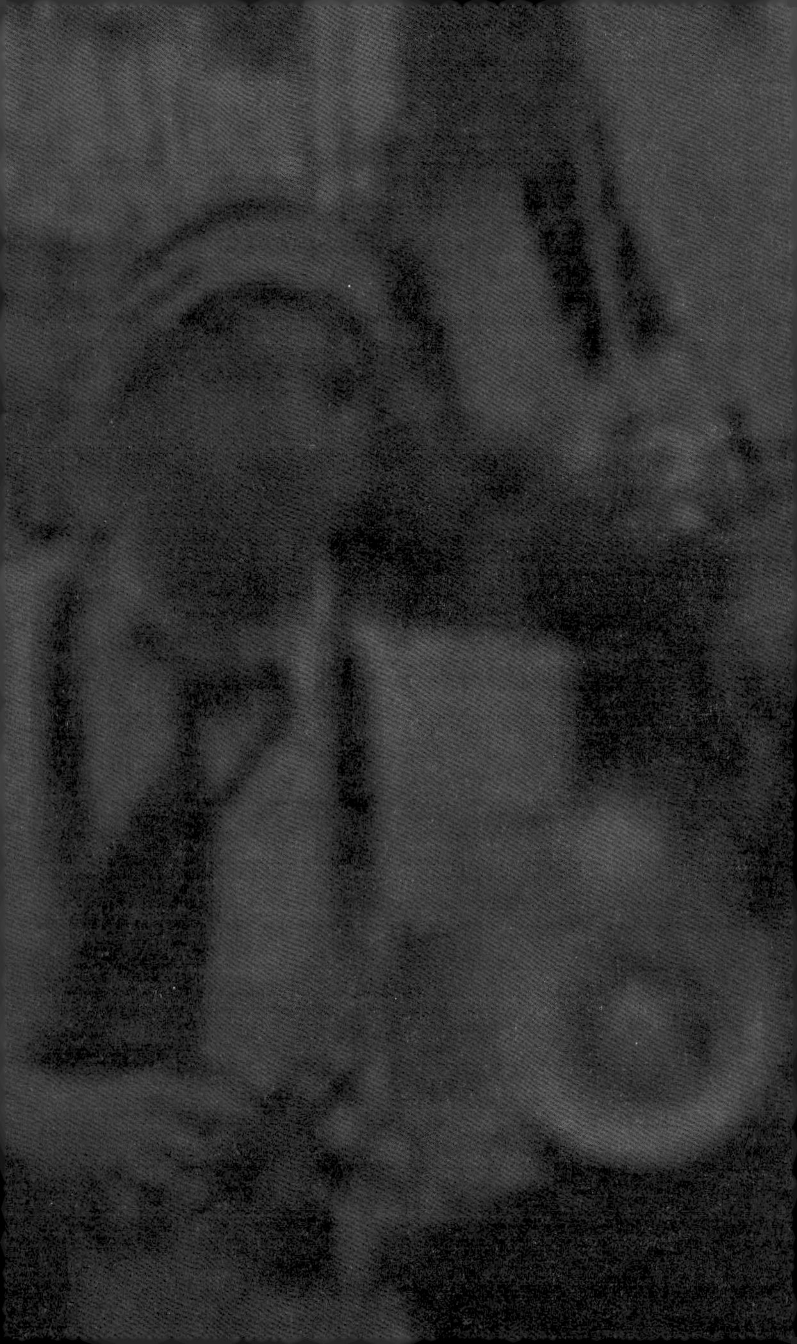

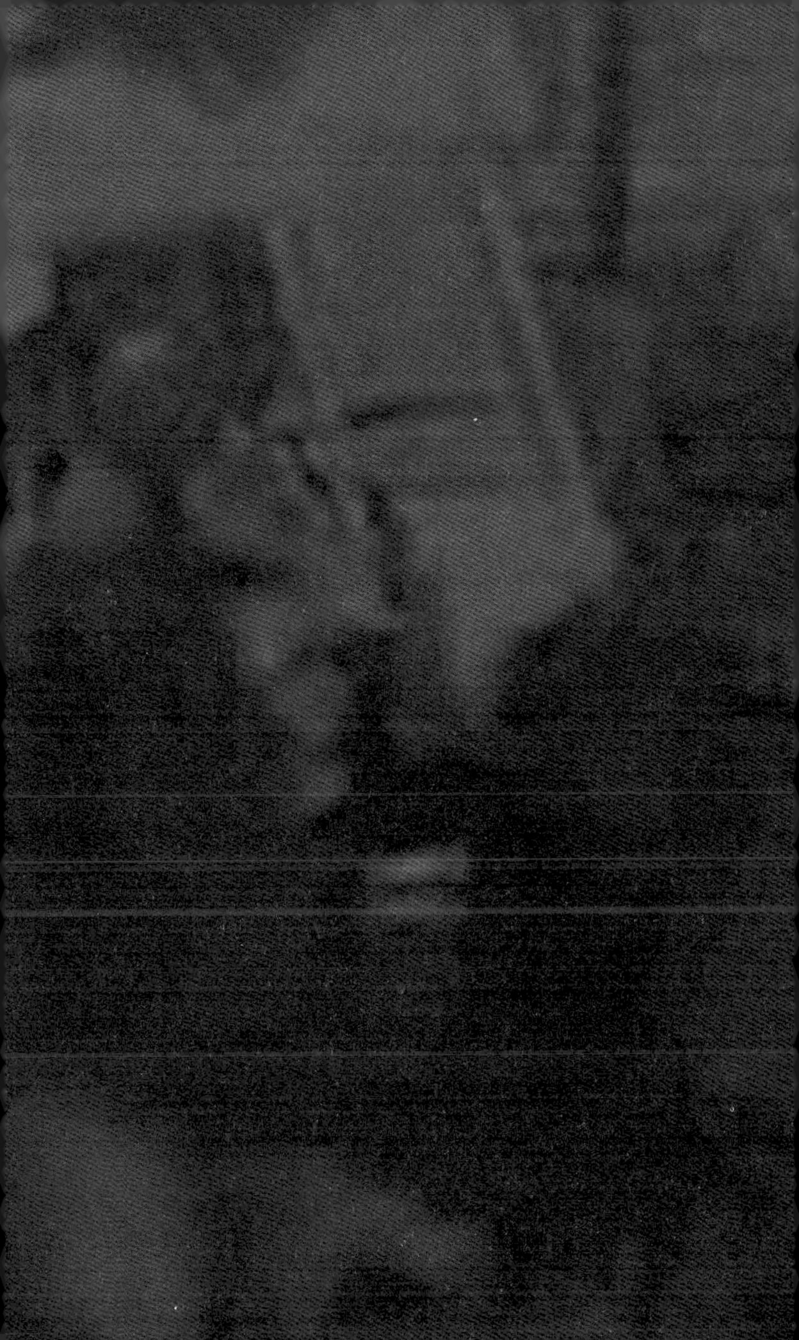

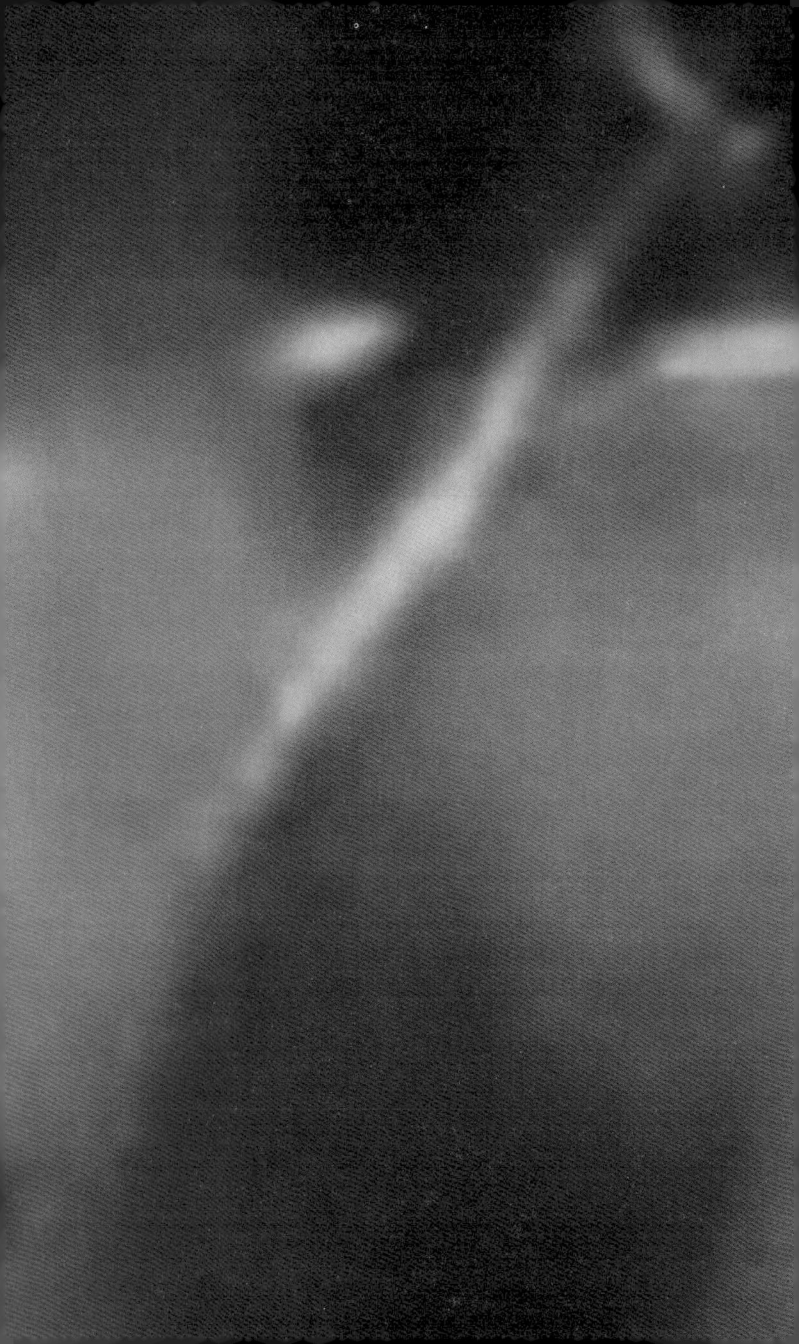

AFTER
CHAPTER IV

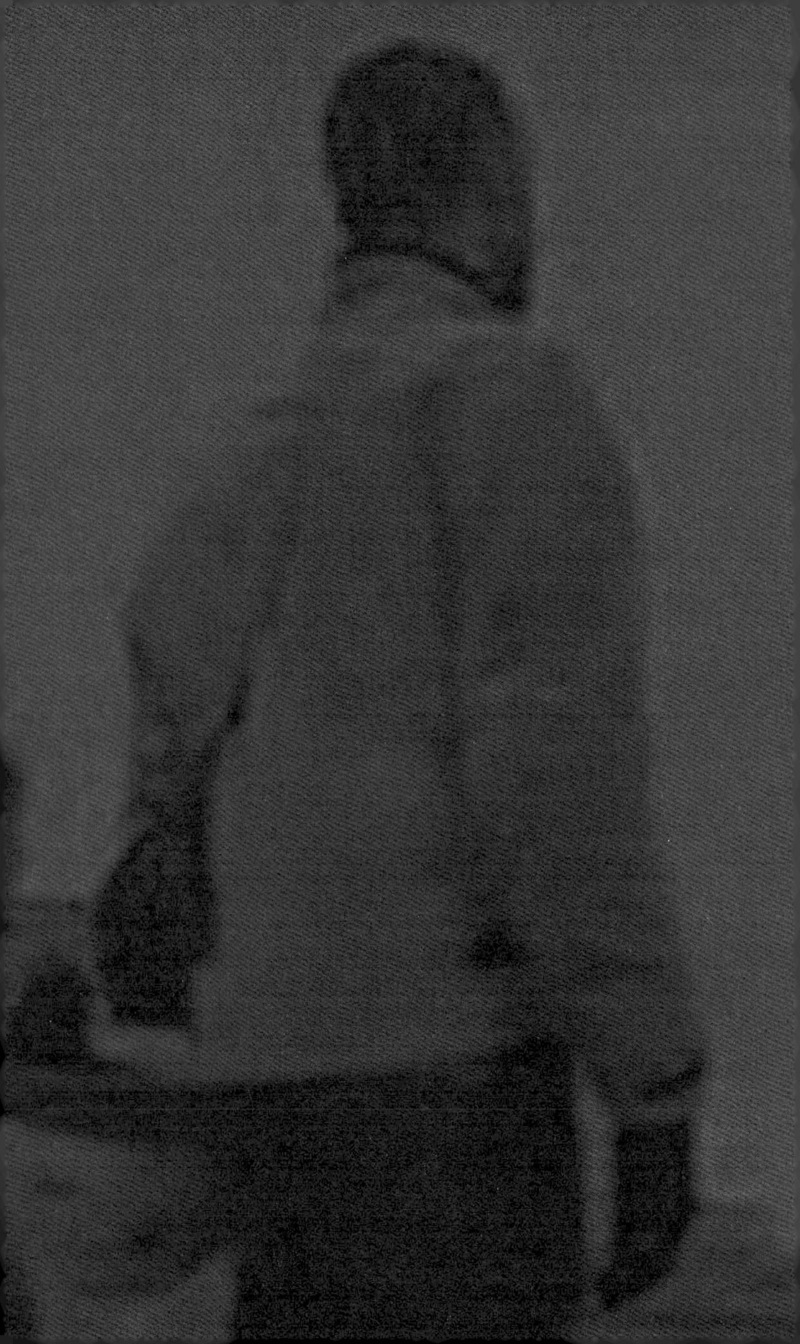

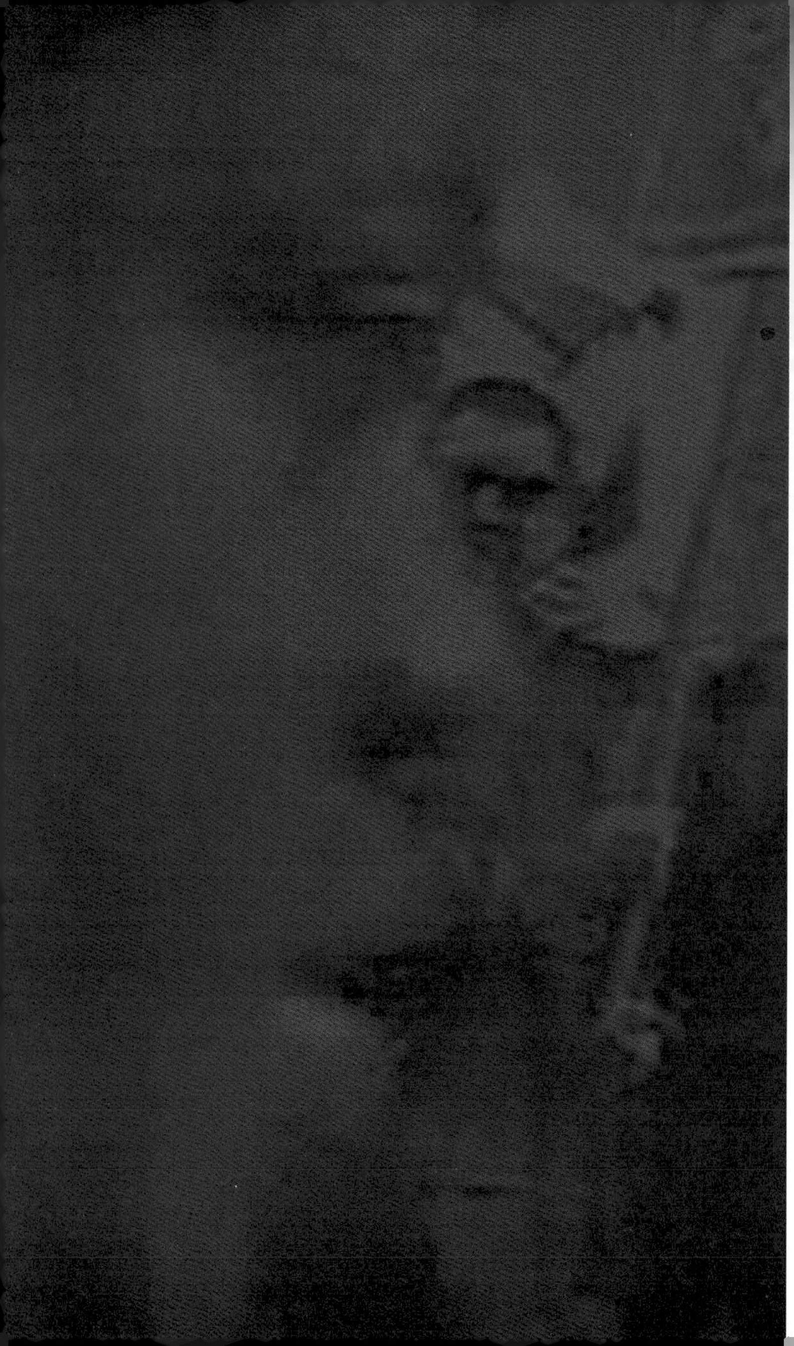

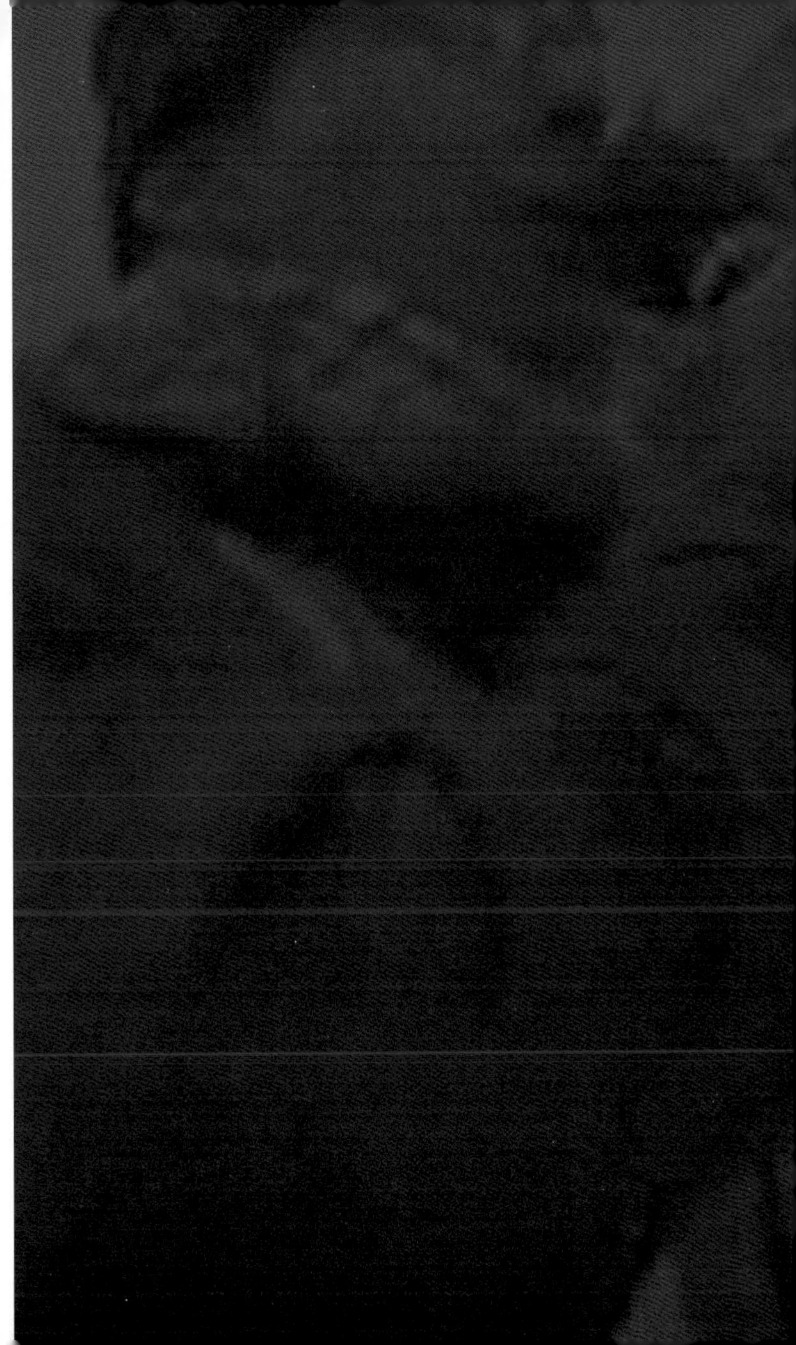

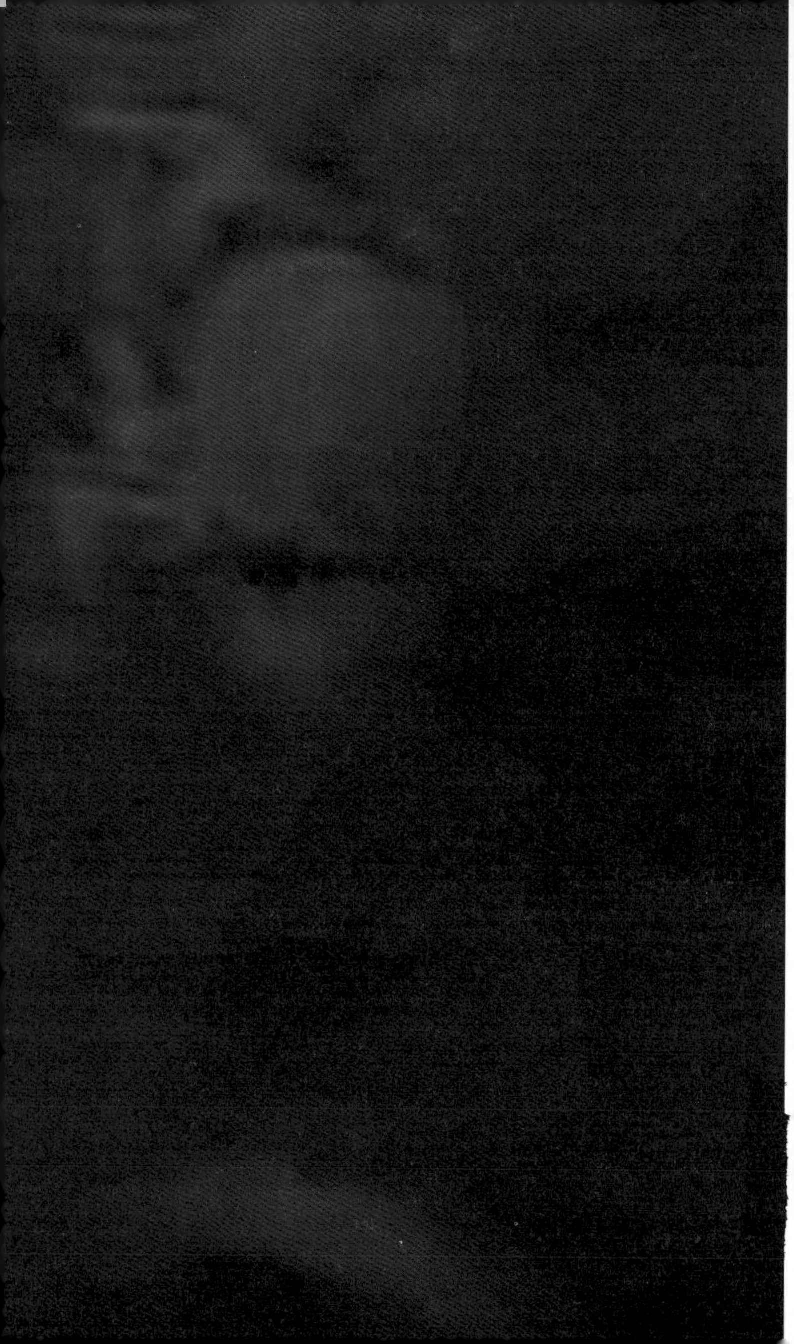

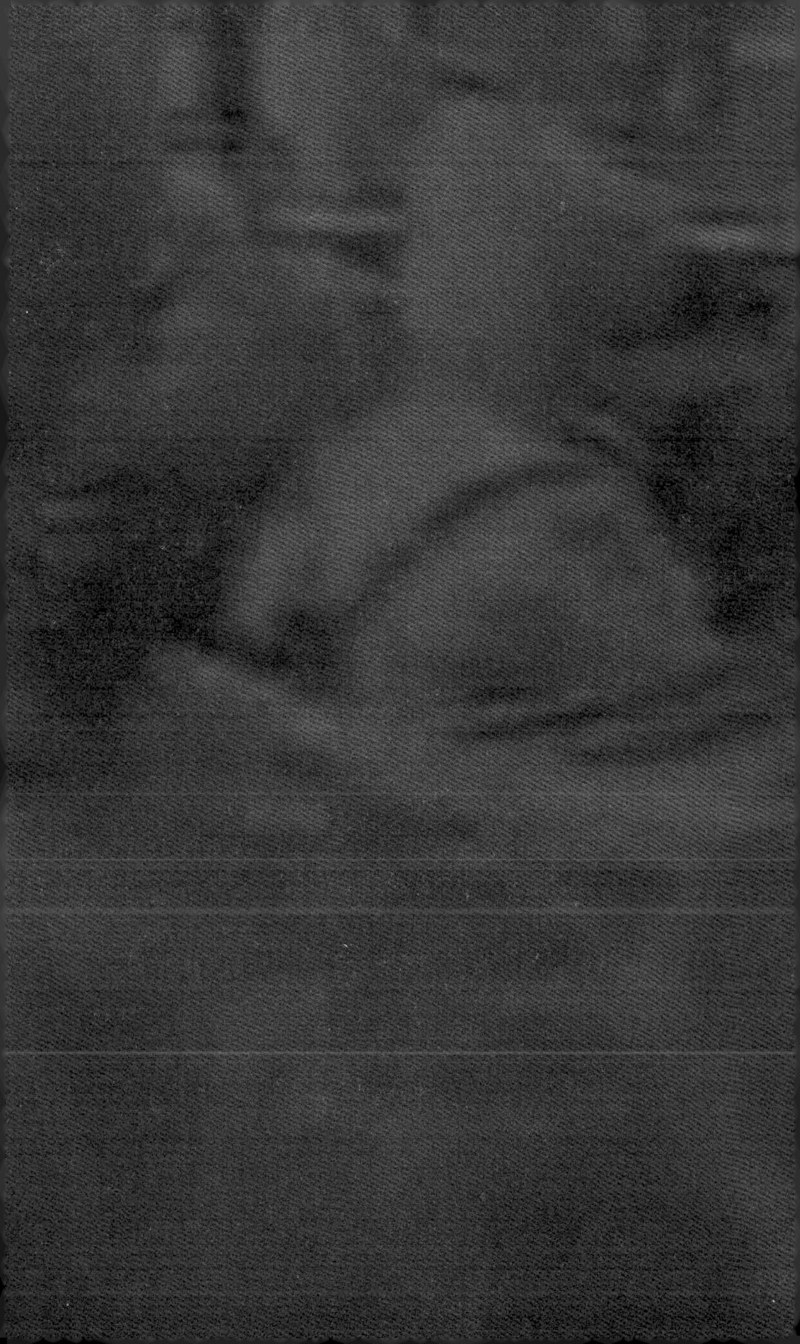

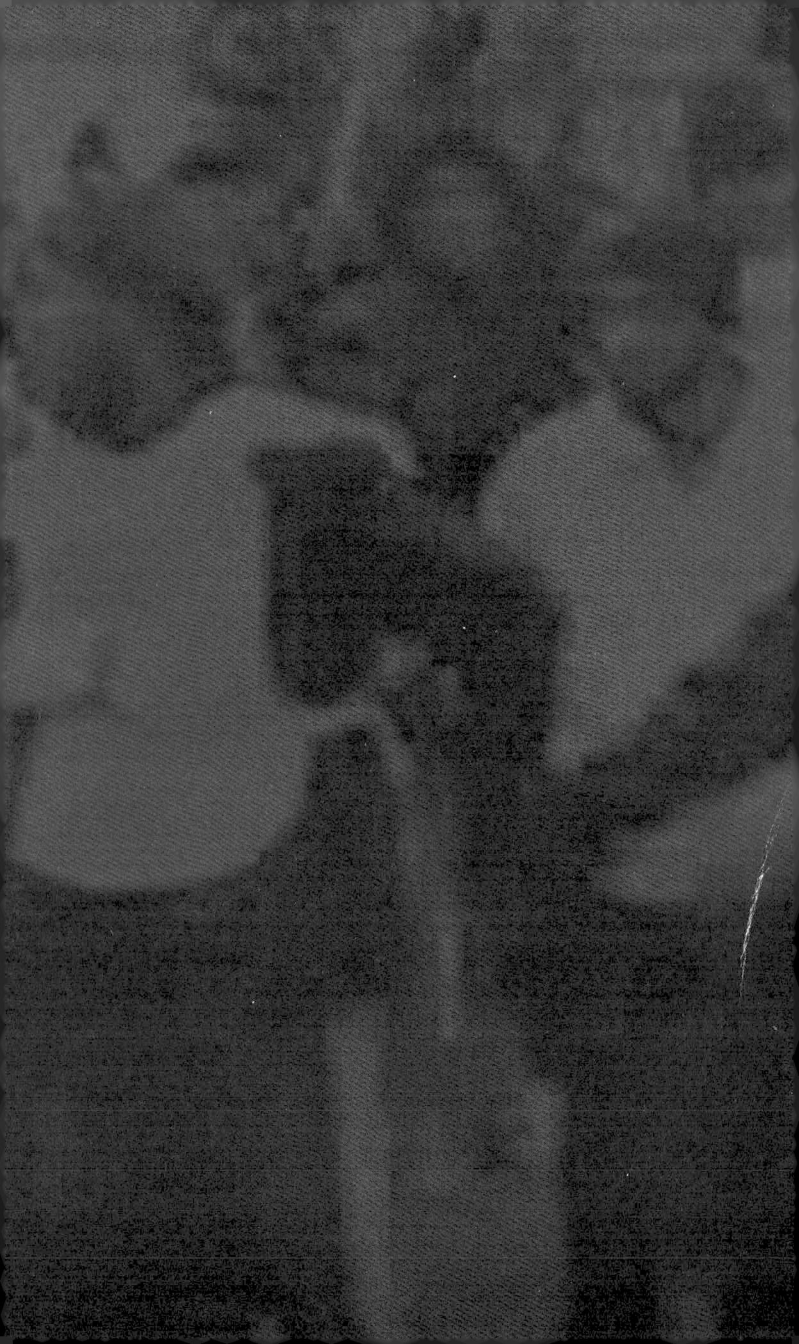

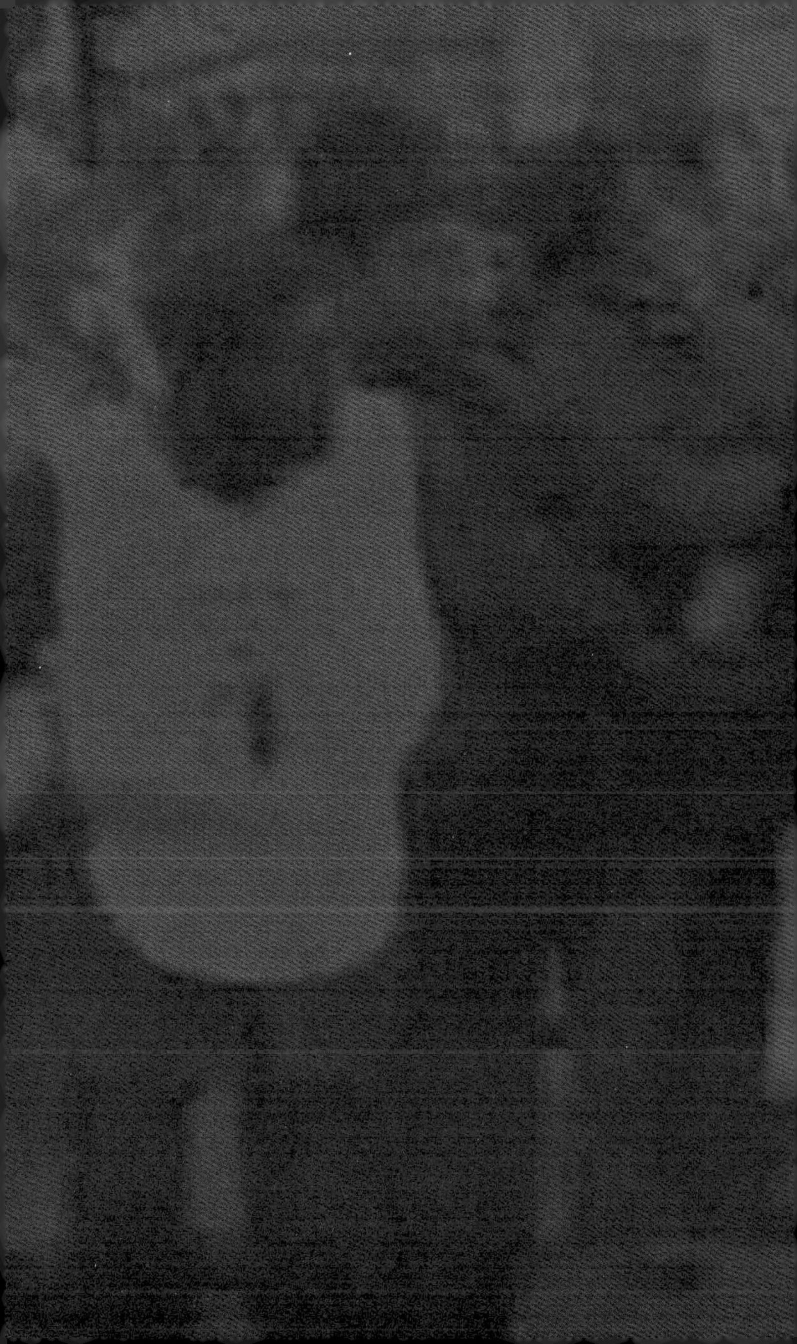

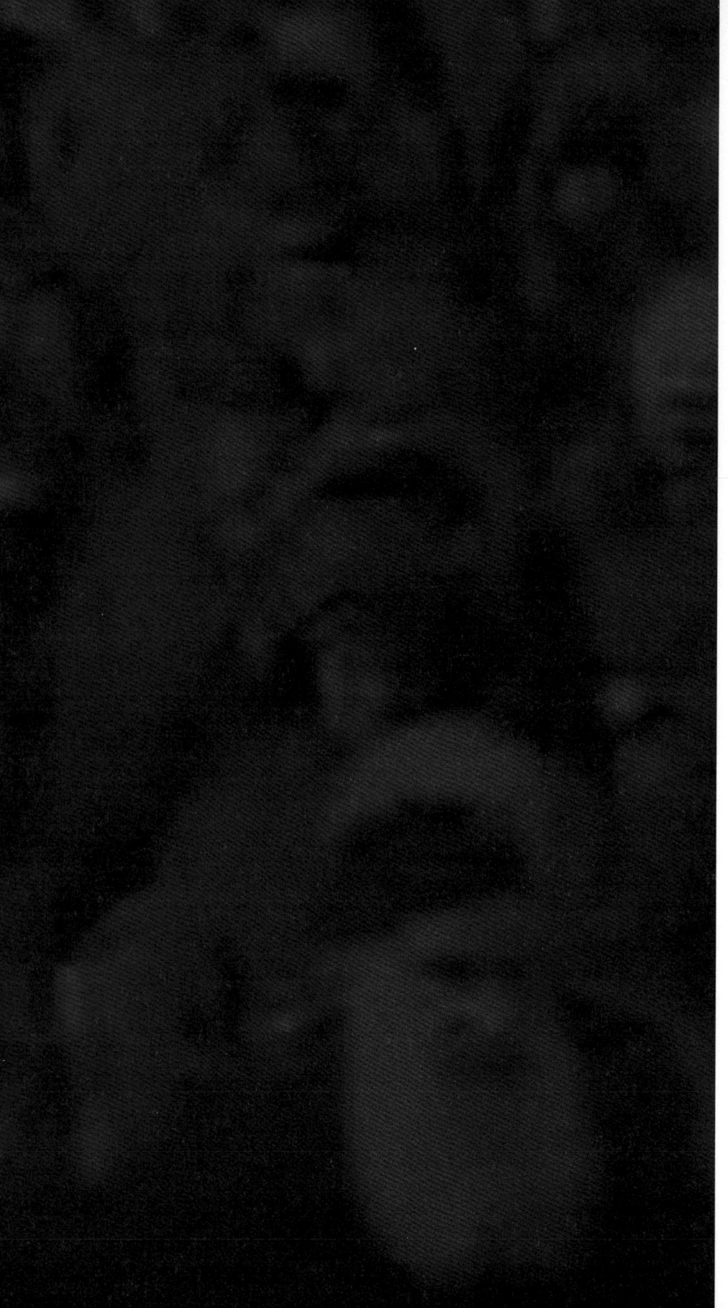

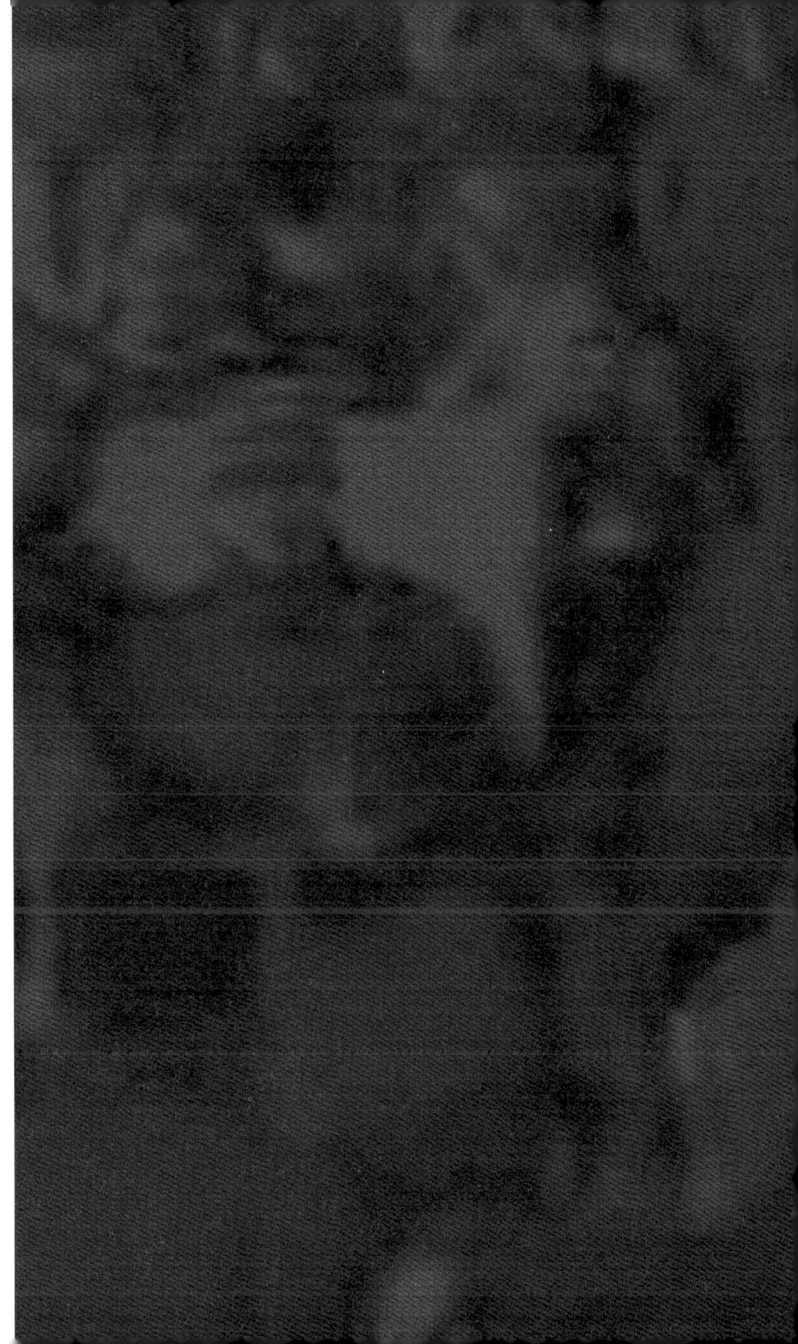

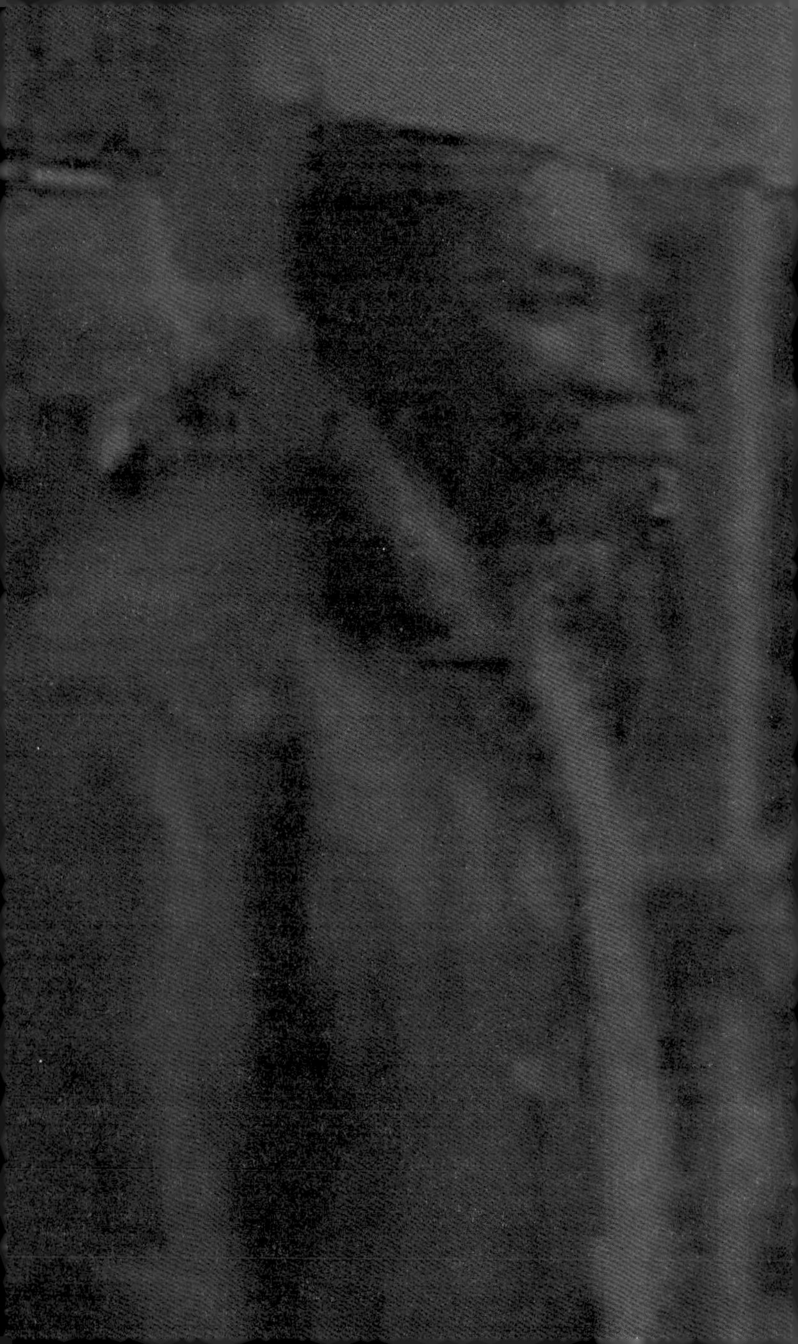

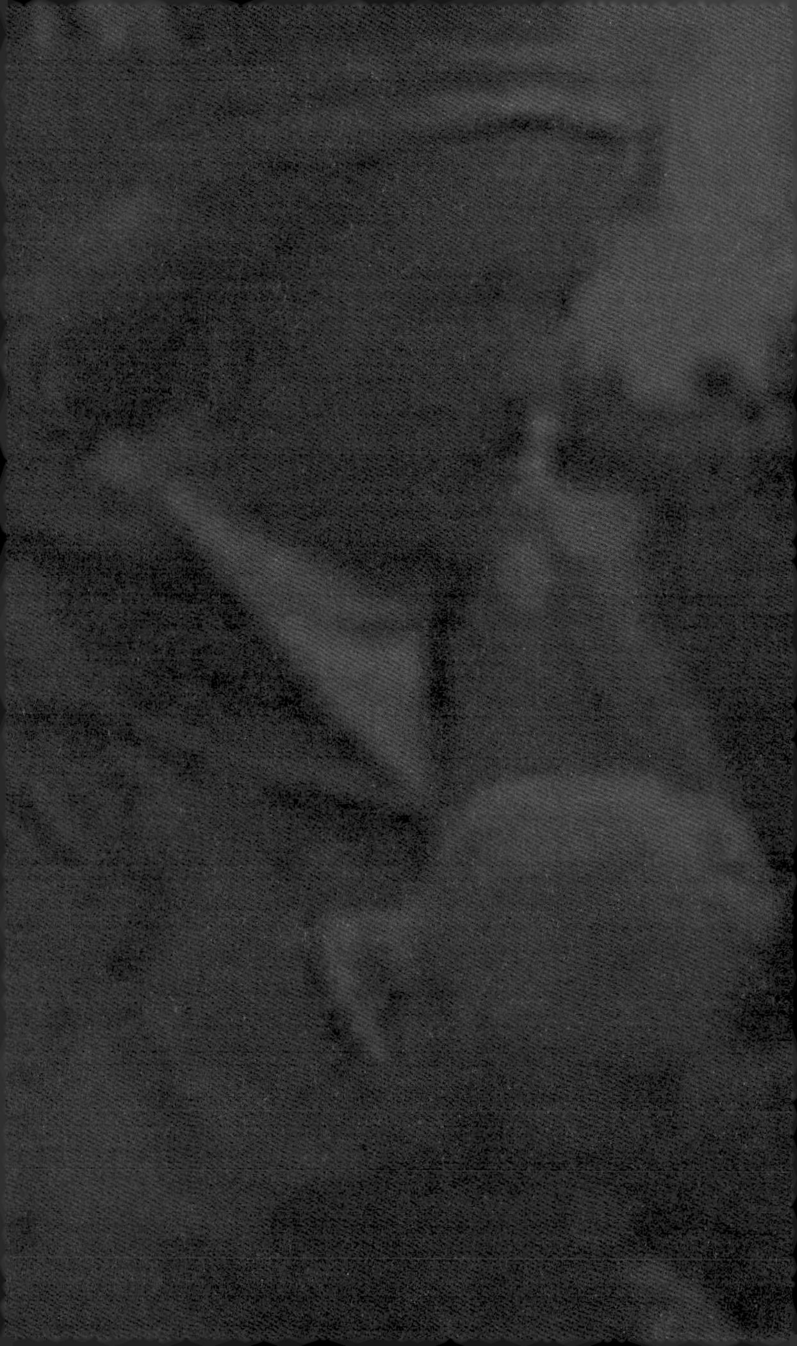

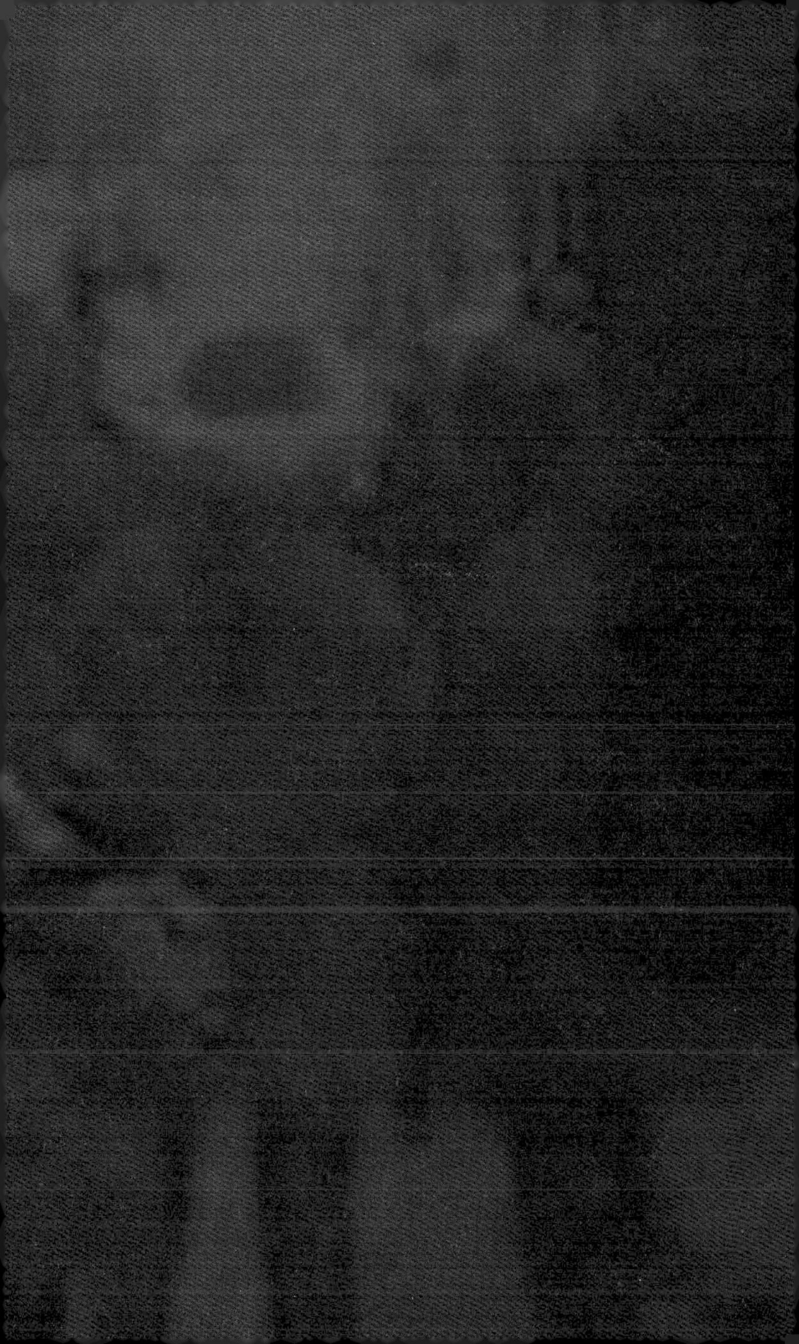

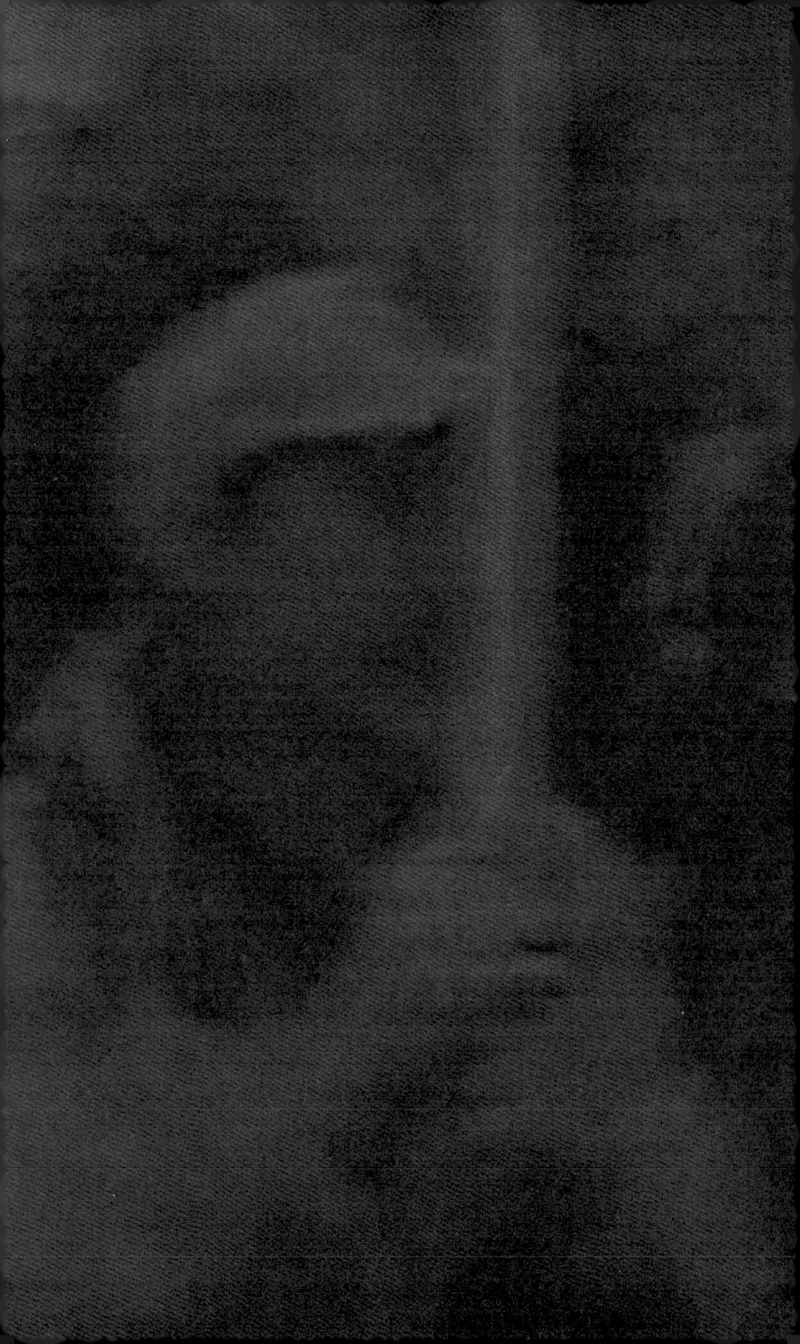

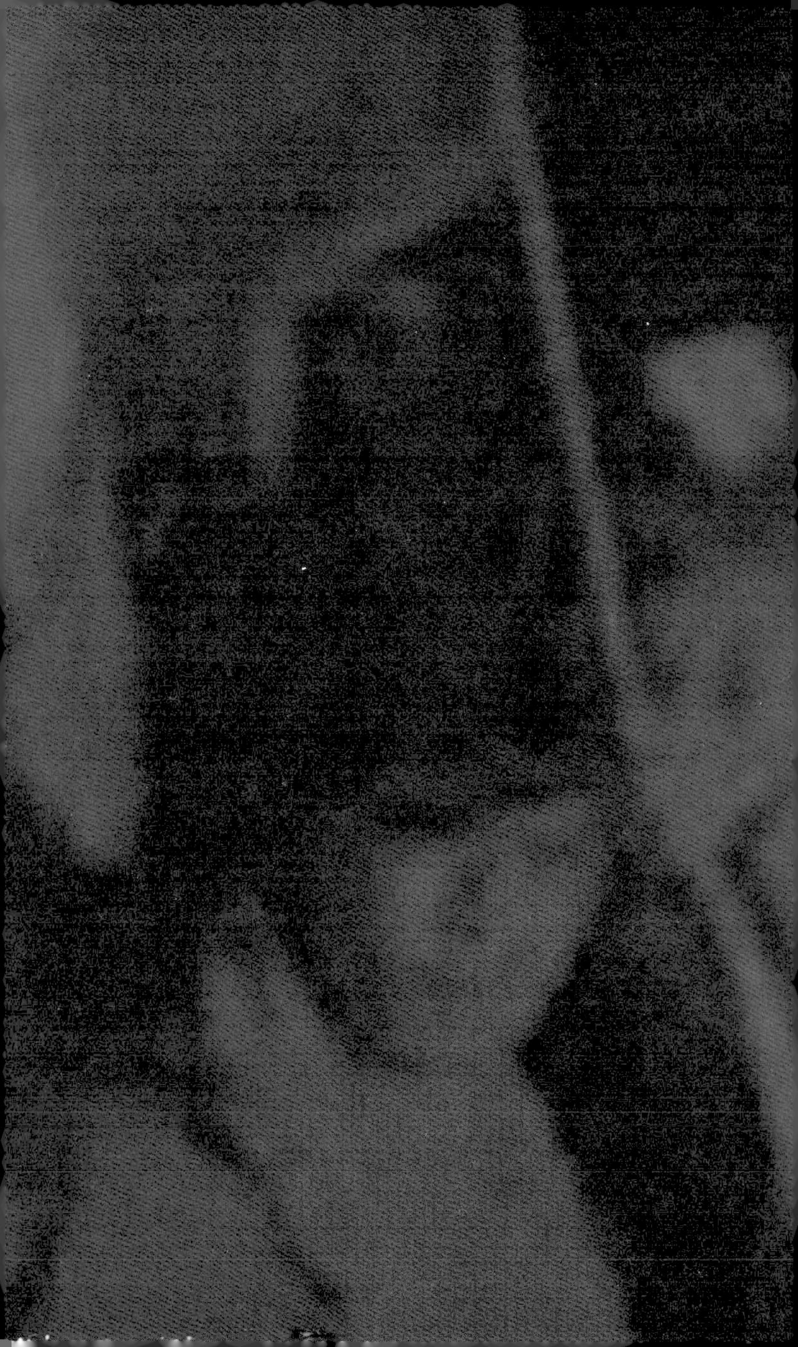

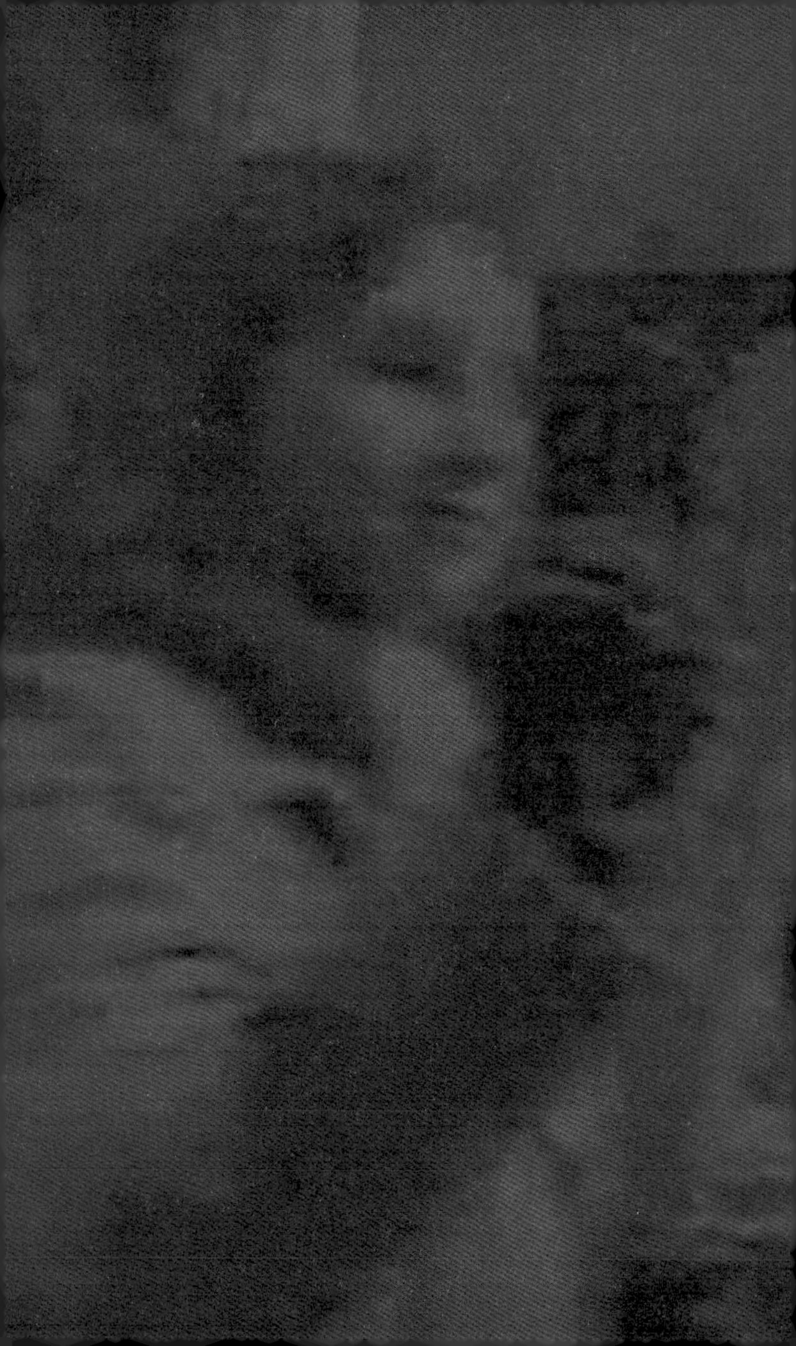

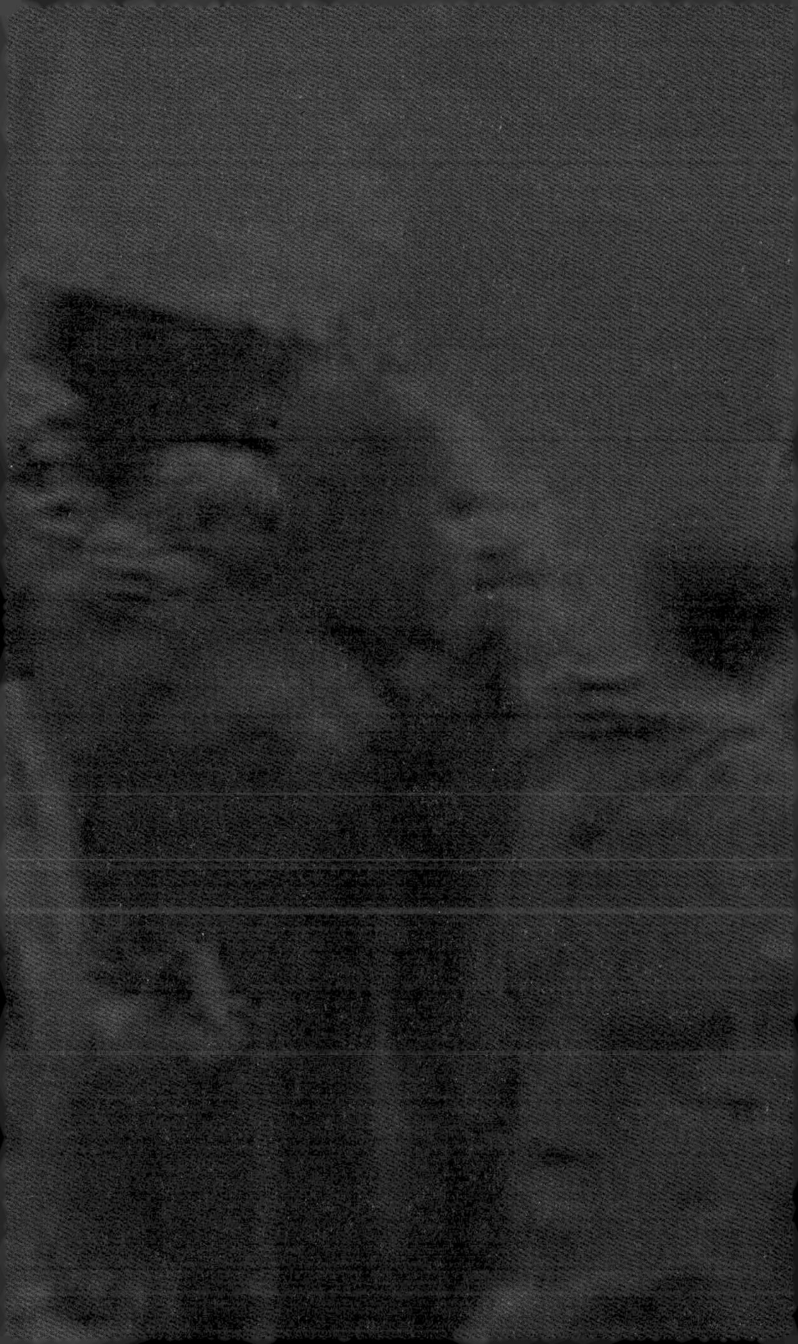

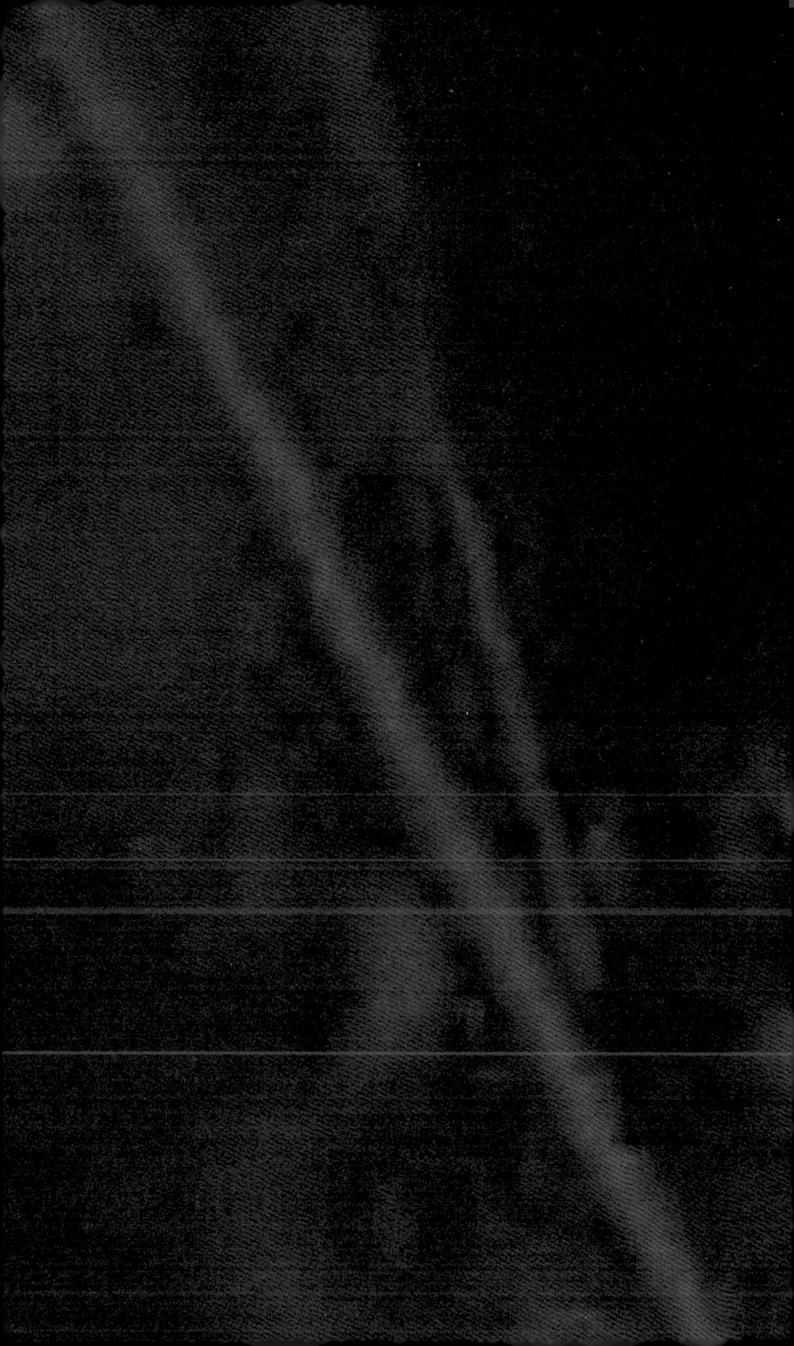

TIME AND AGAIN

CHAPTER V

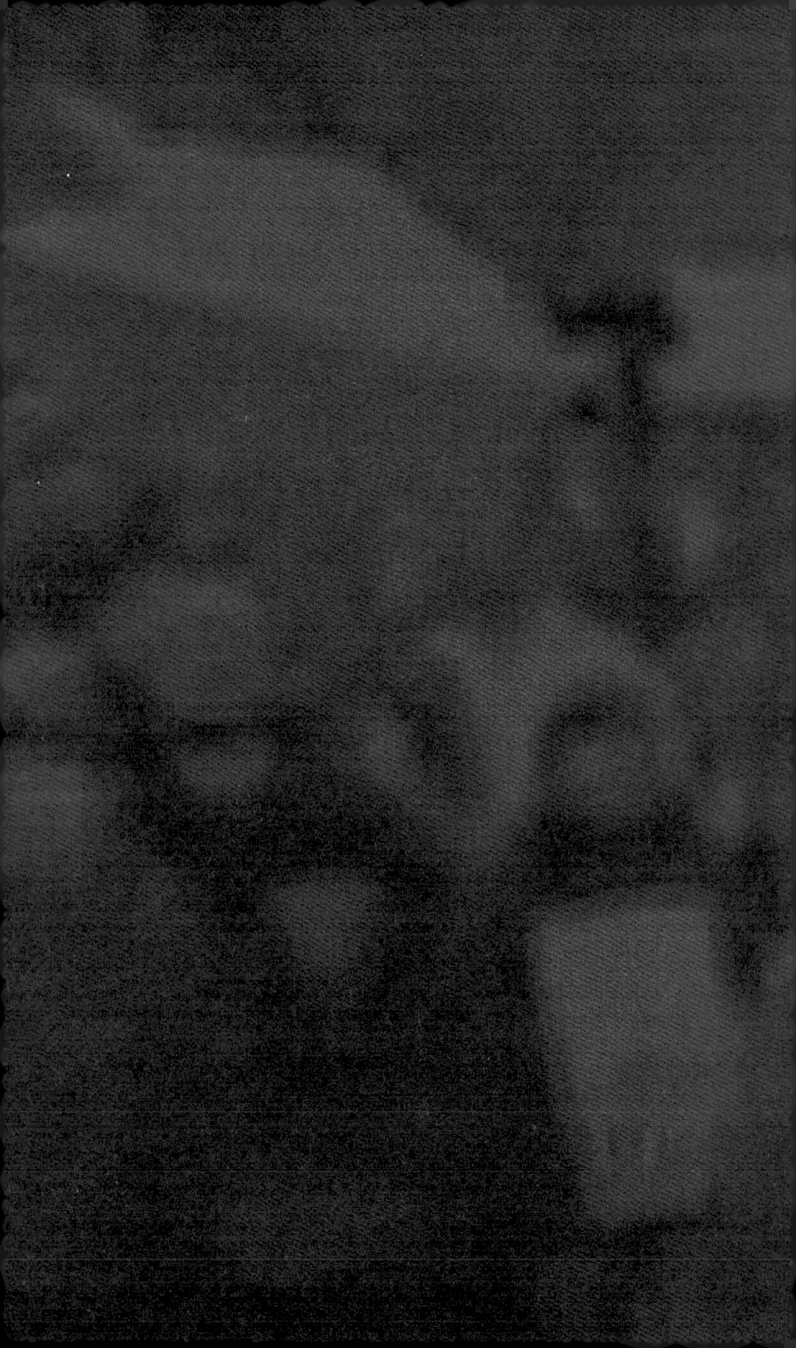

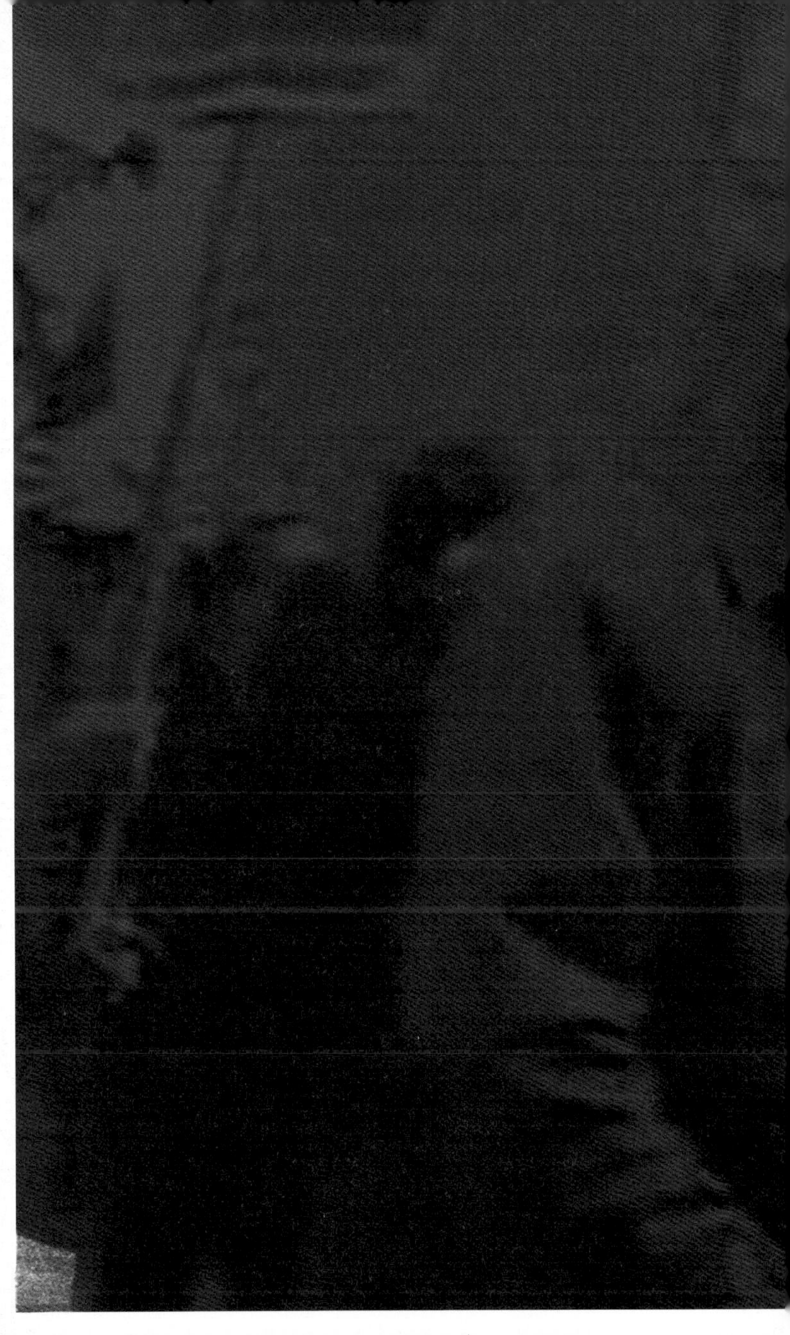

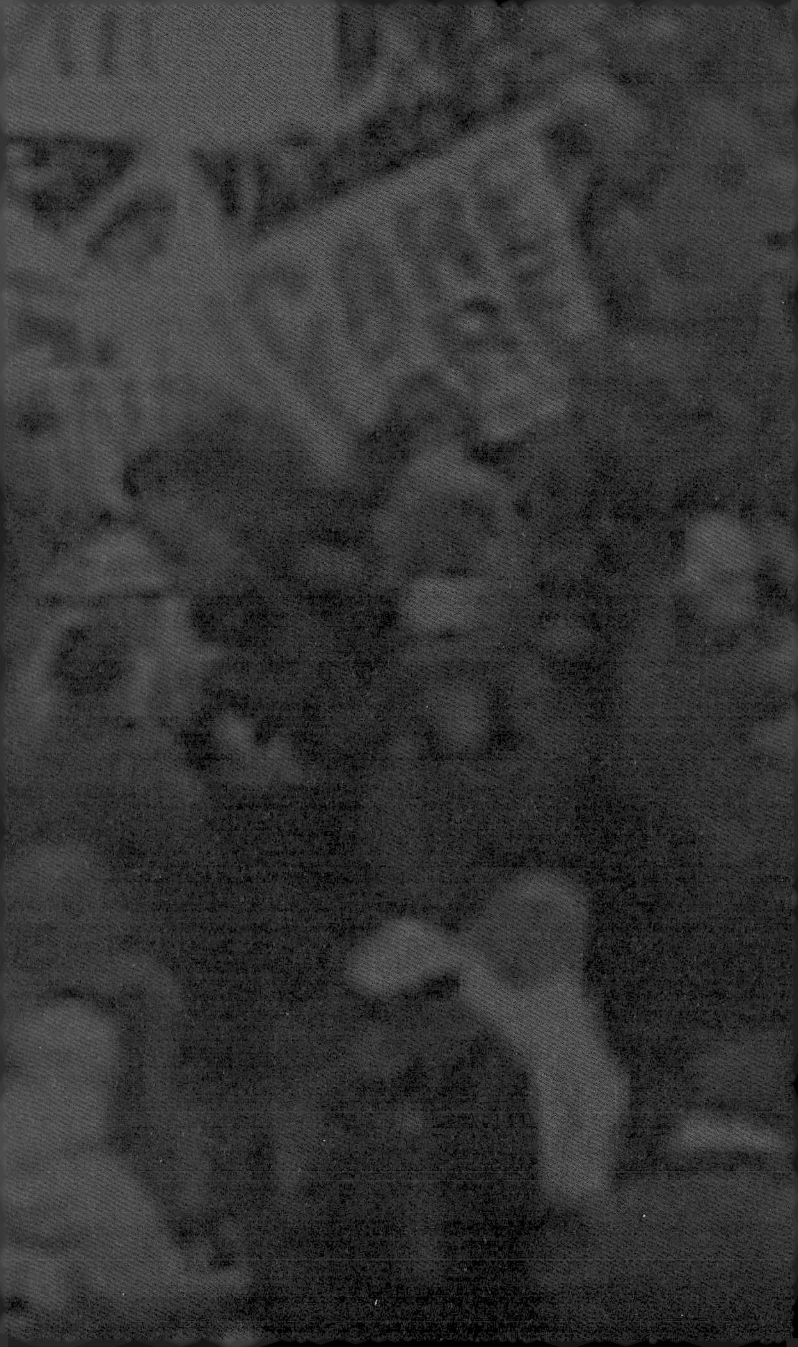

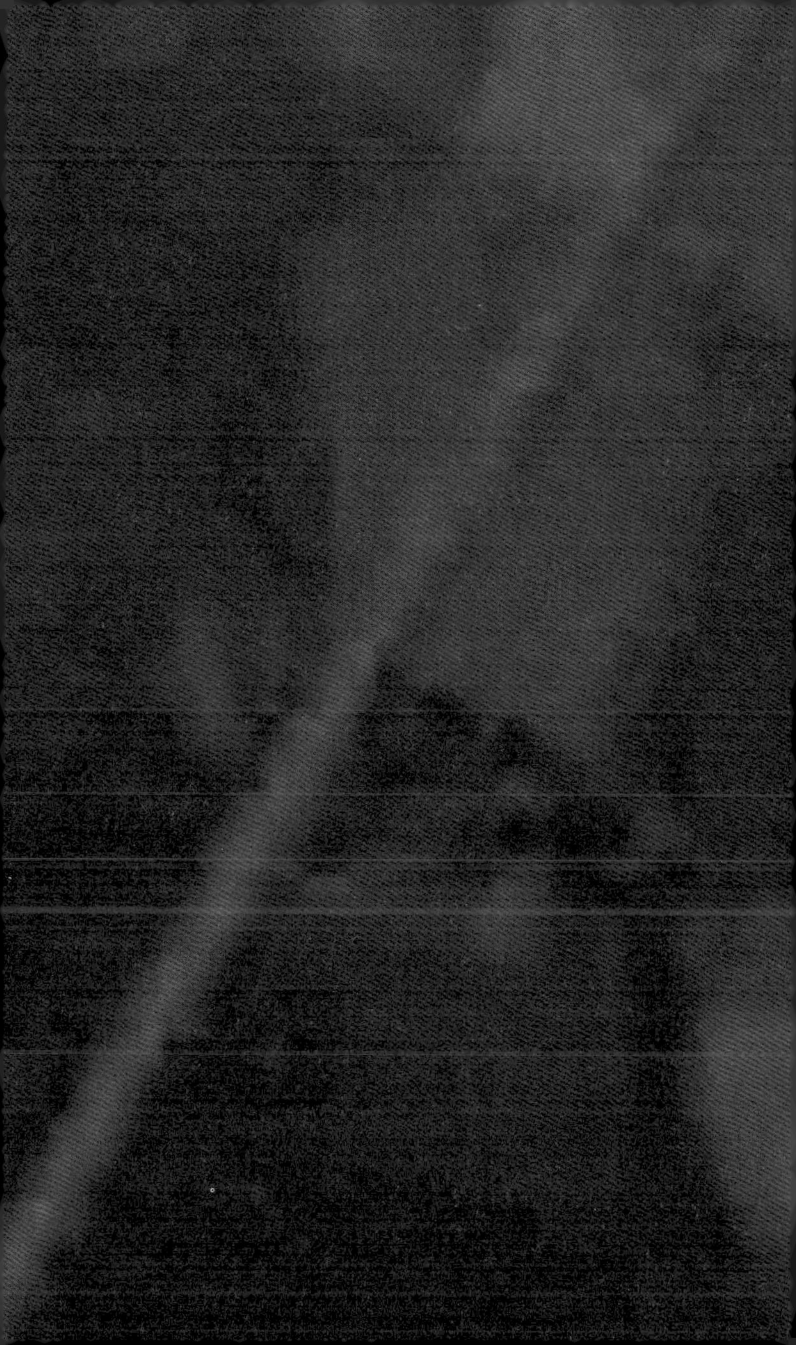

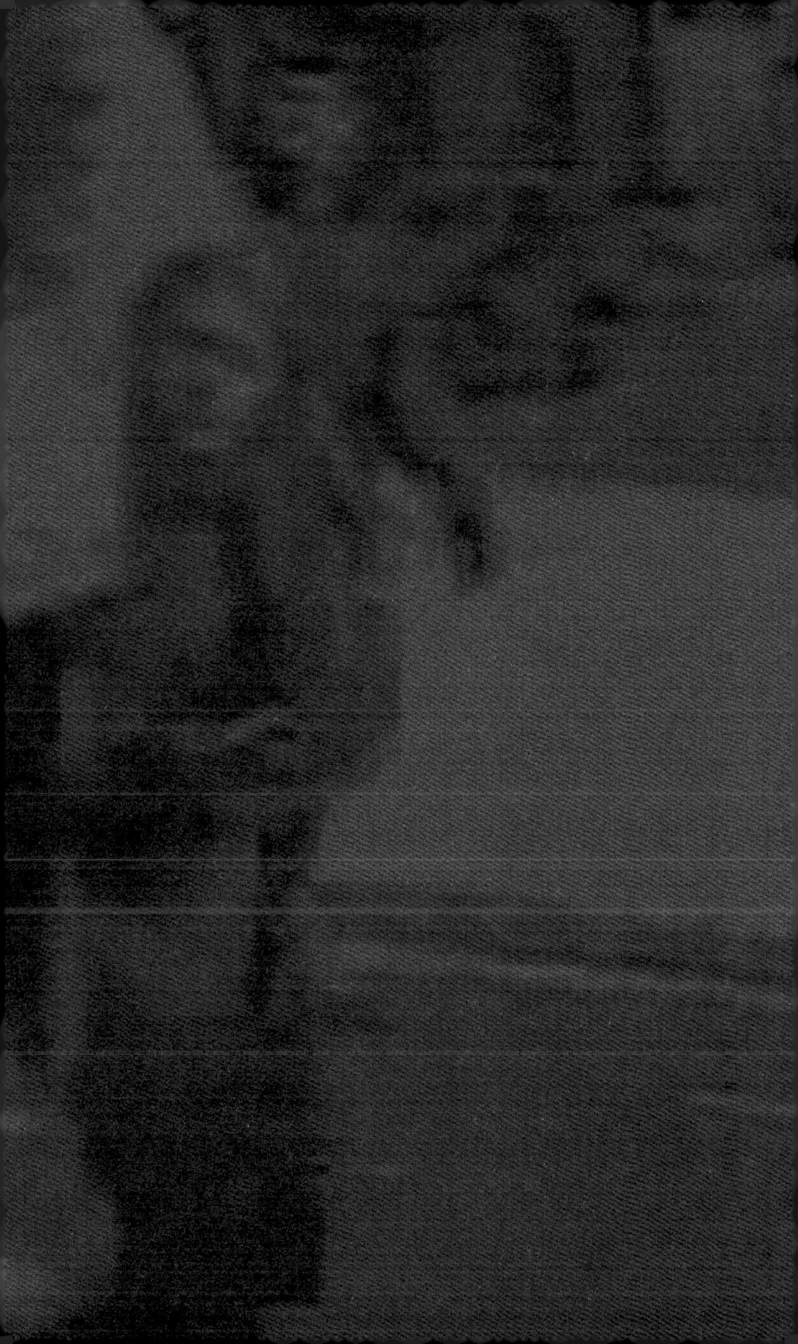

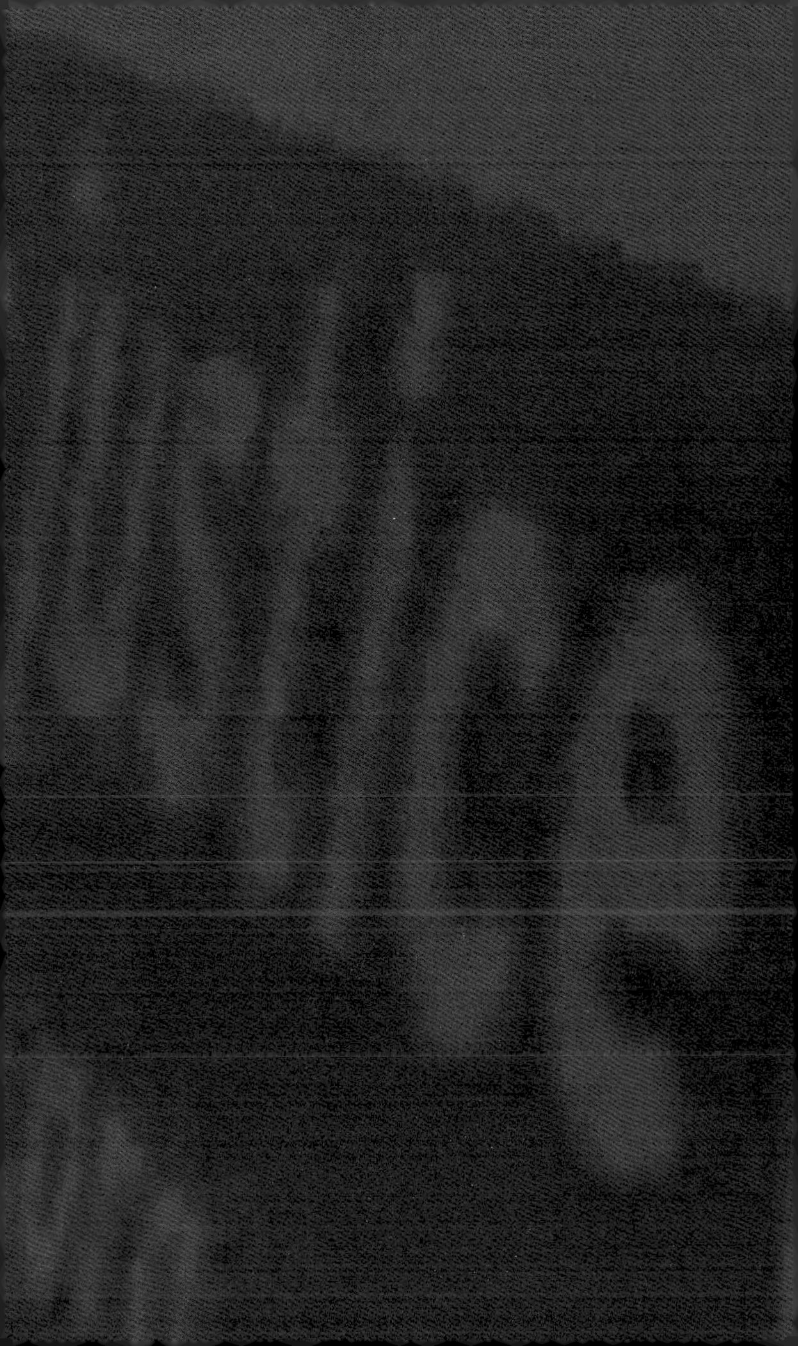

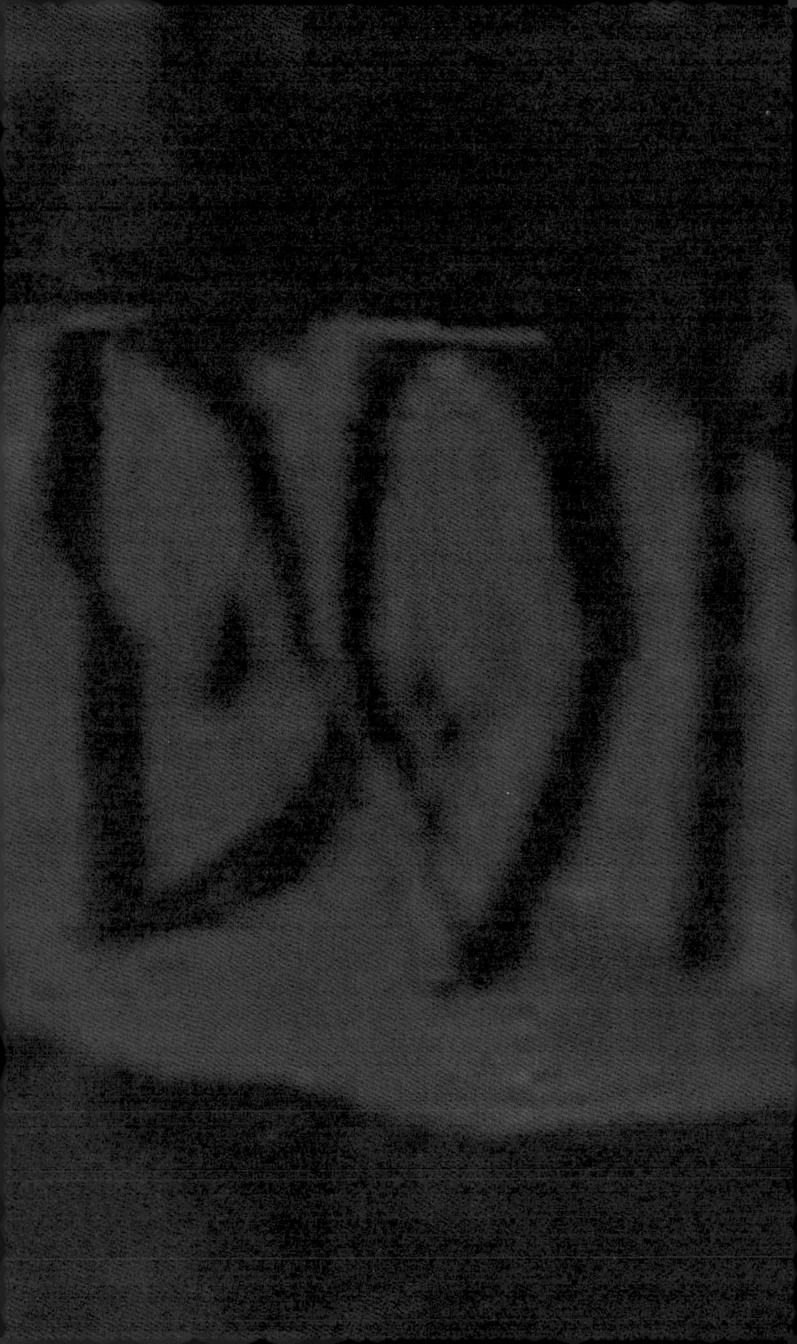

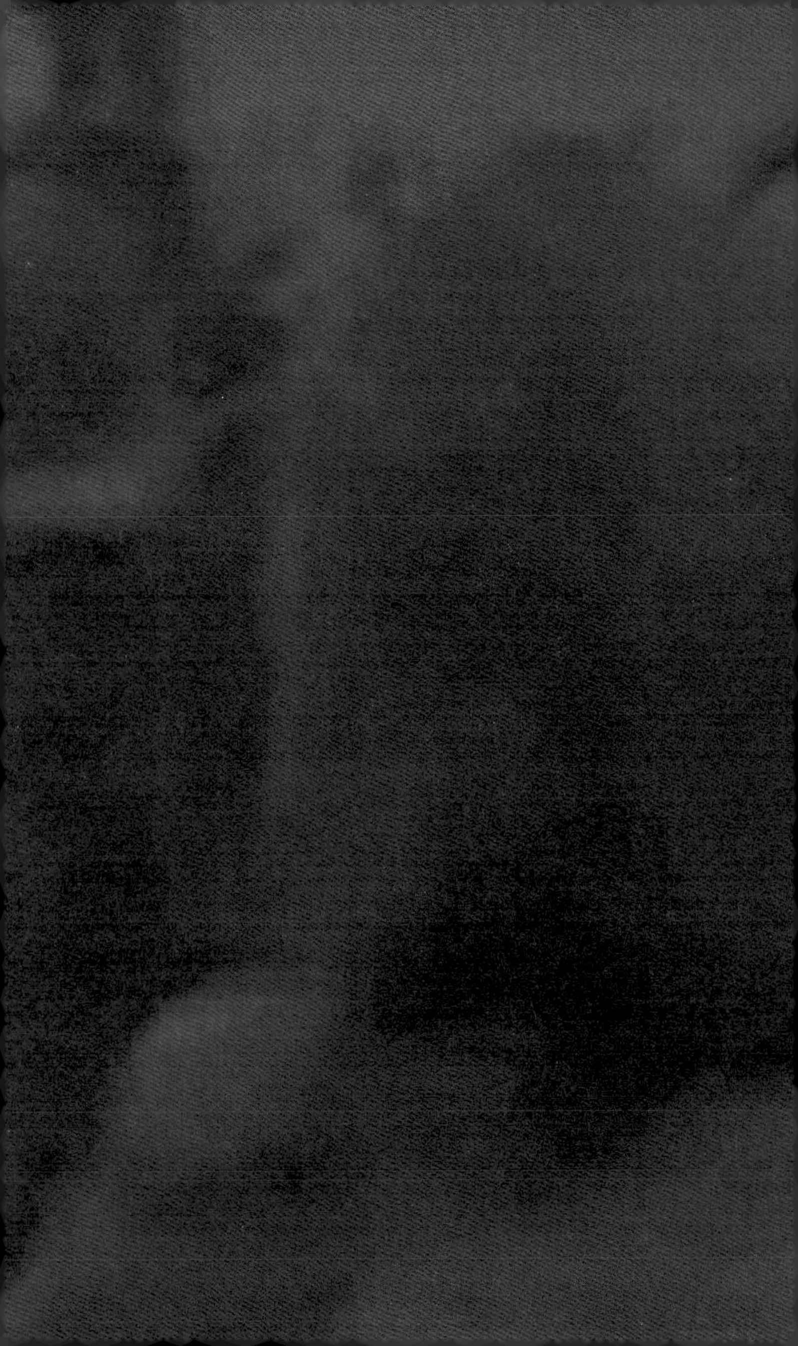

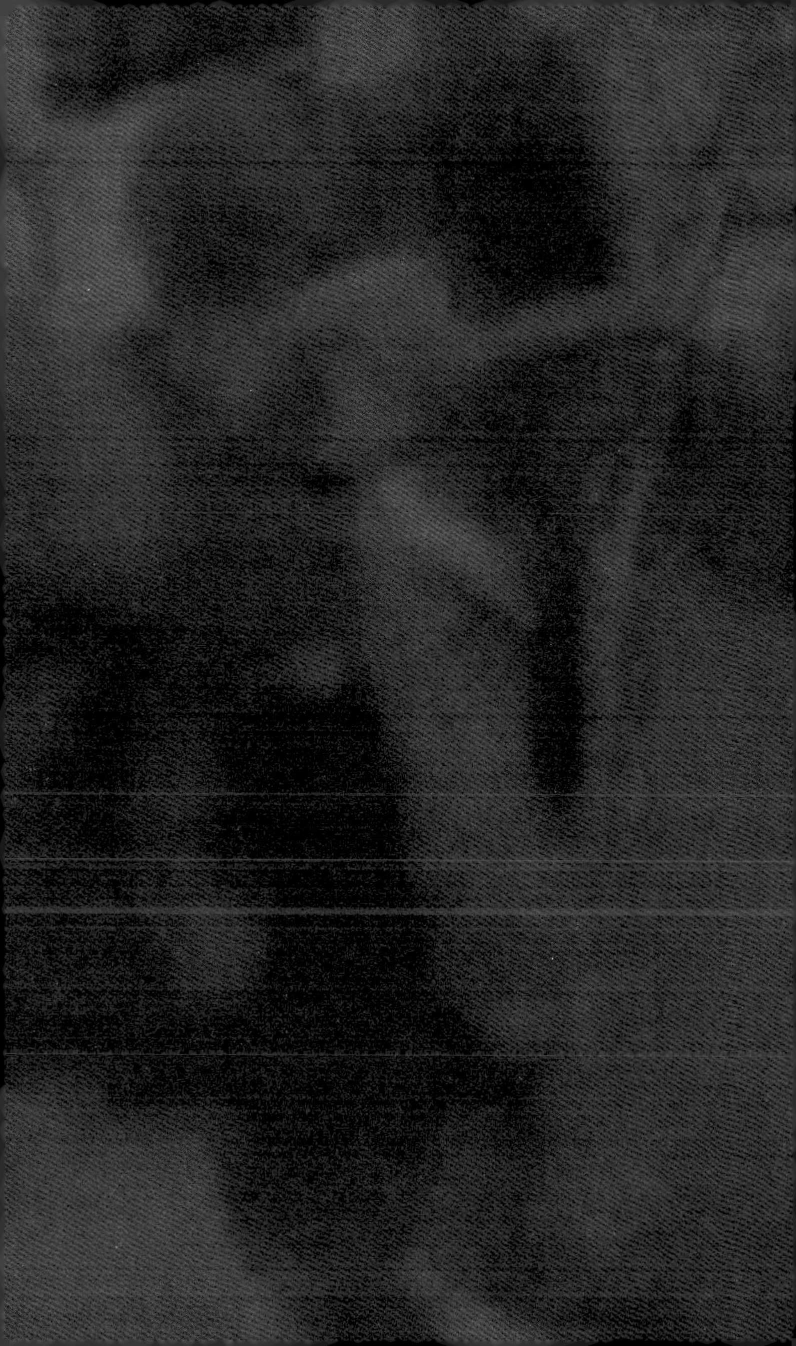

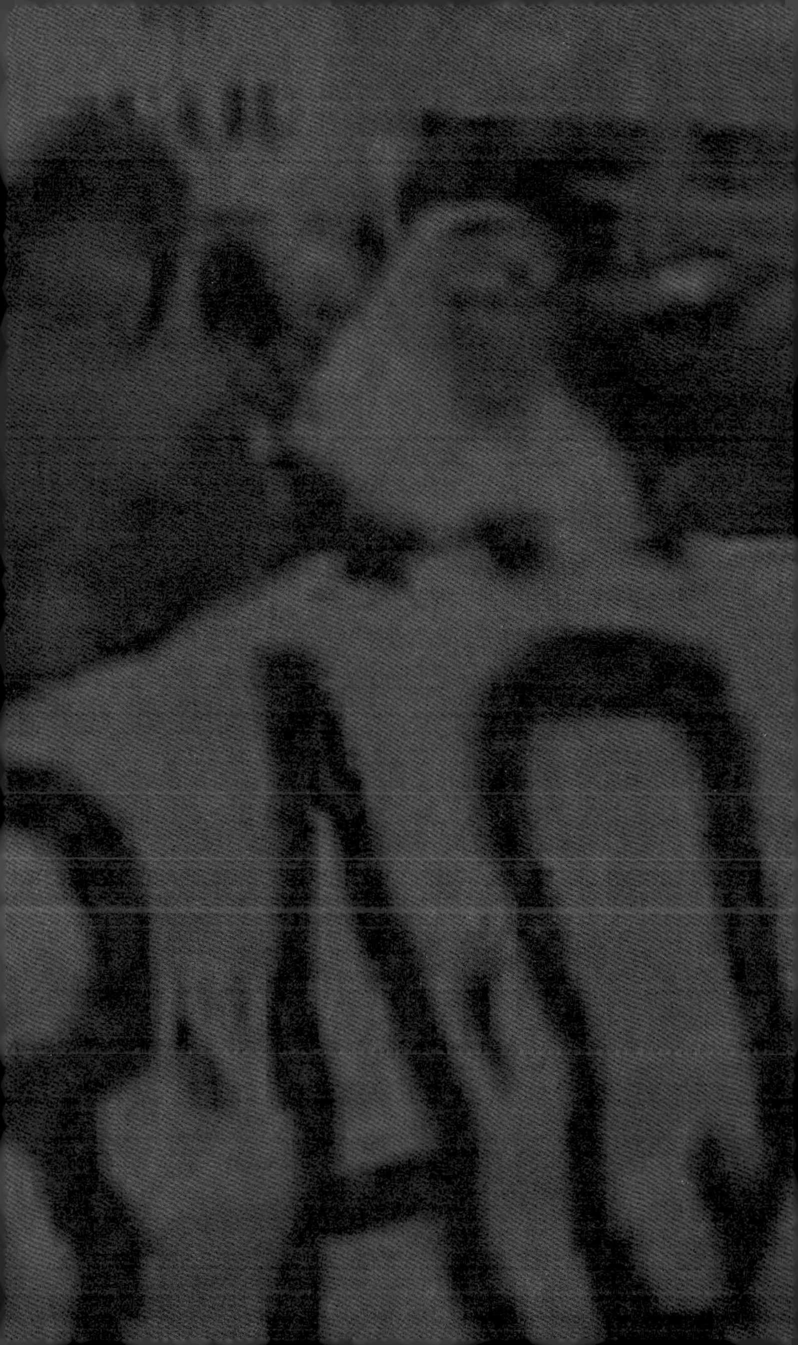

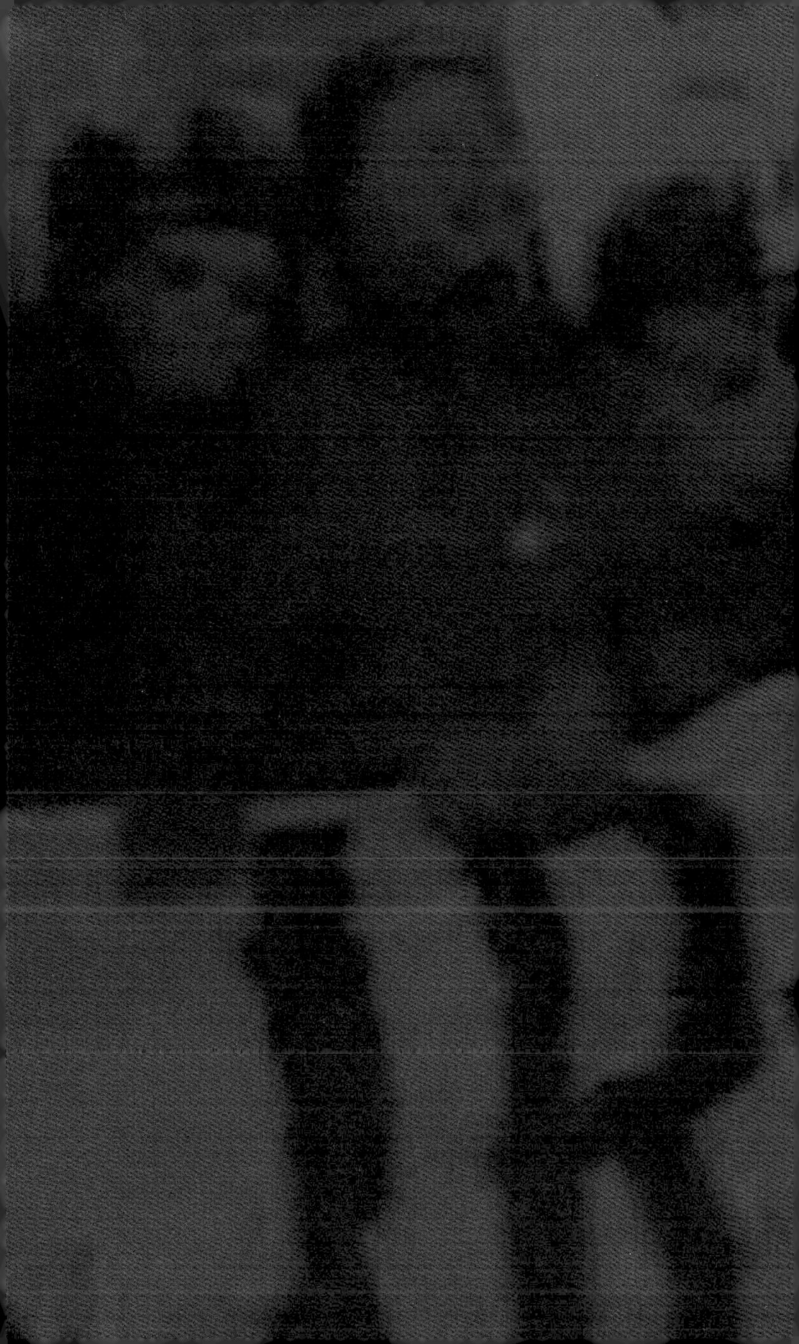

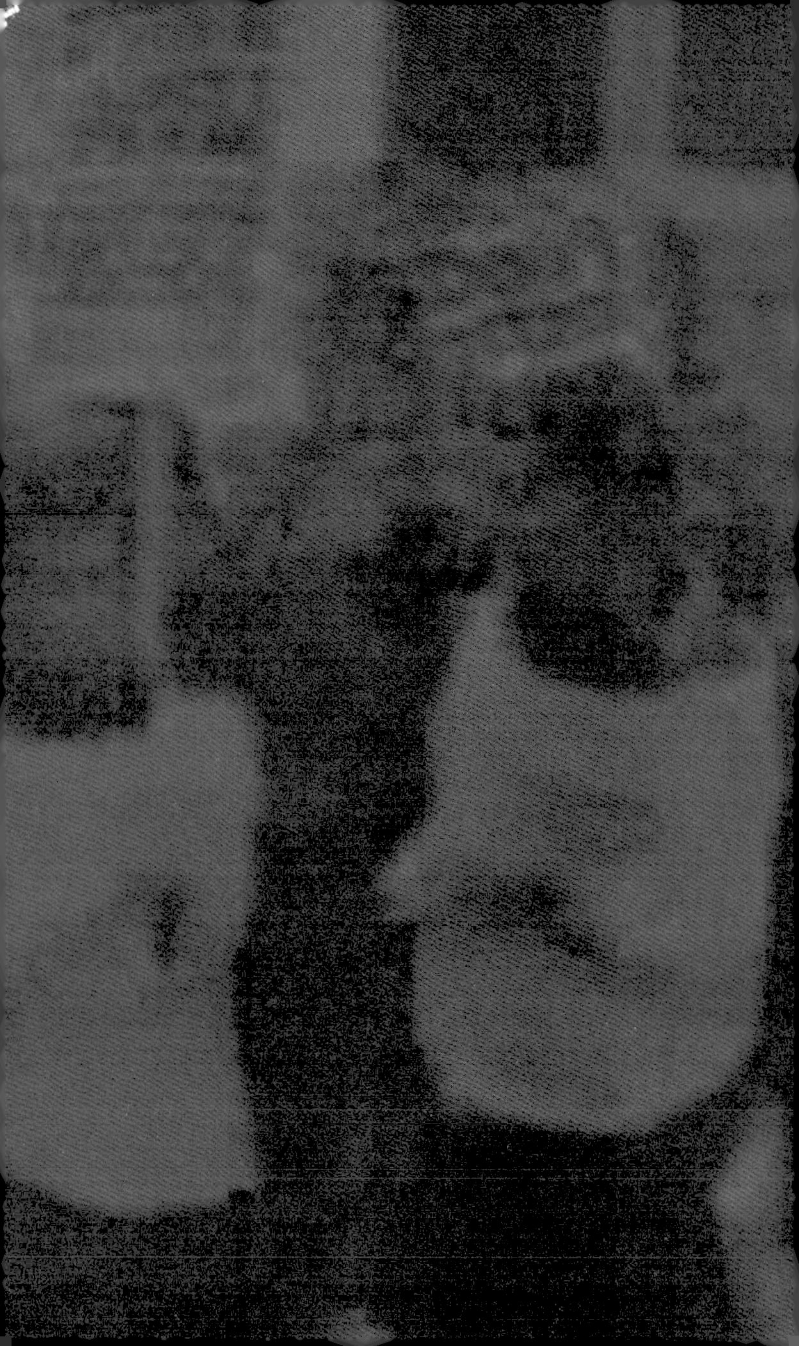

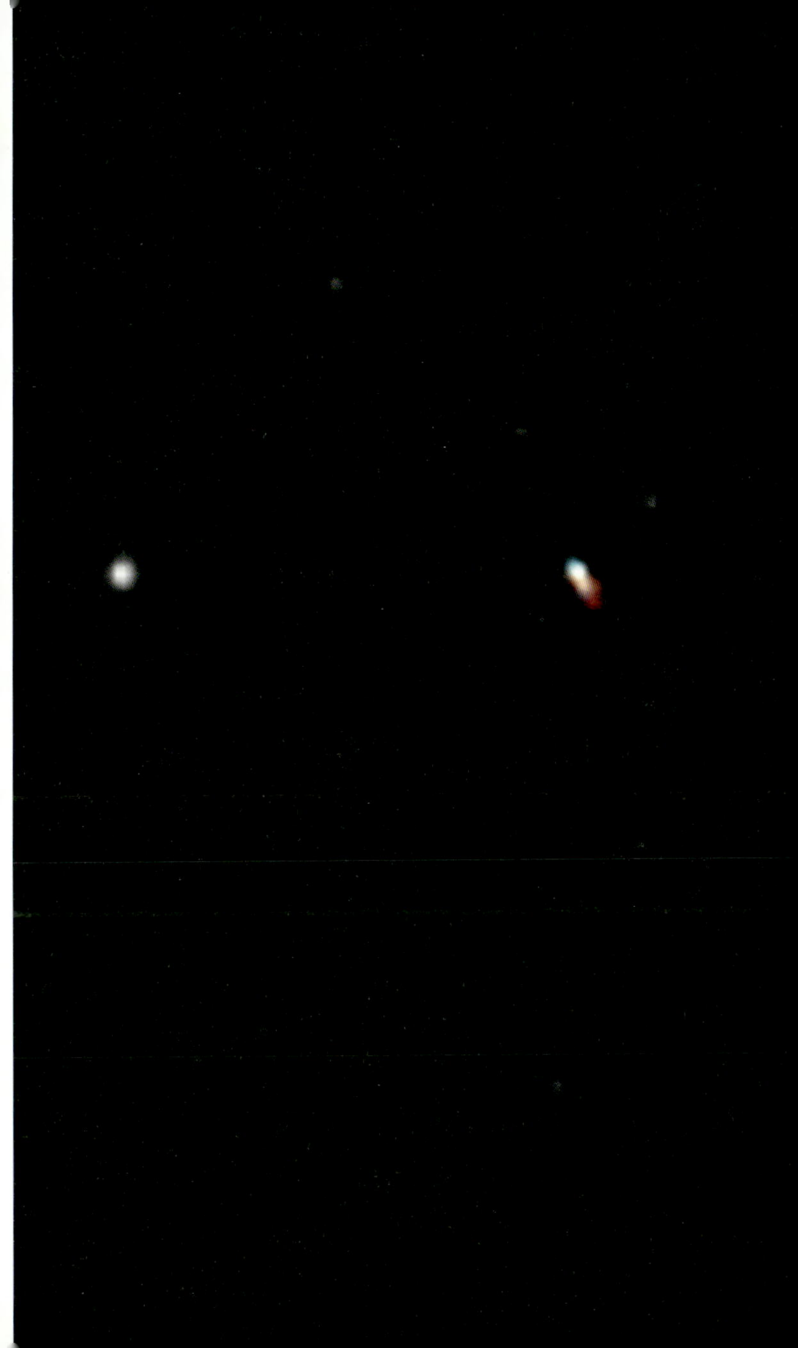

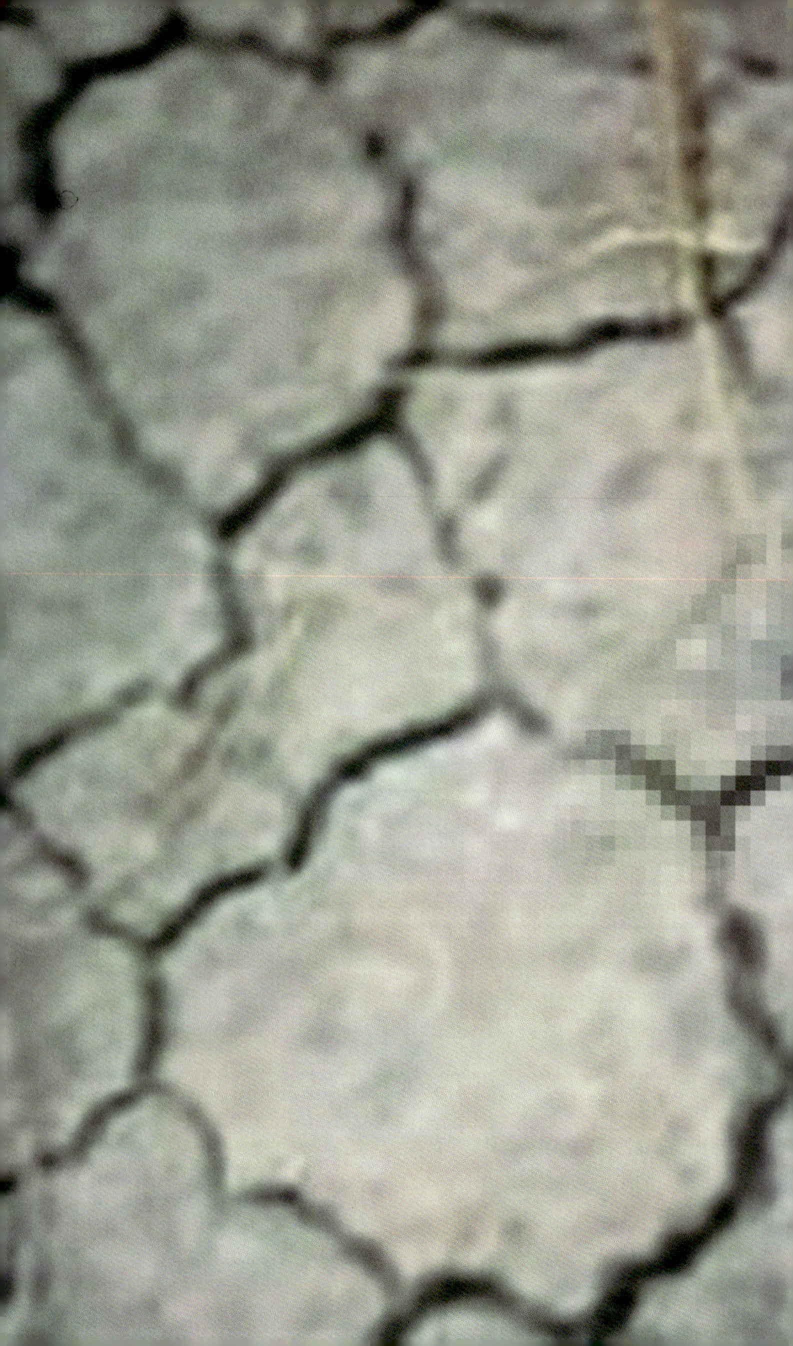

BEFORE

CHAPTER VI

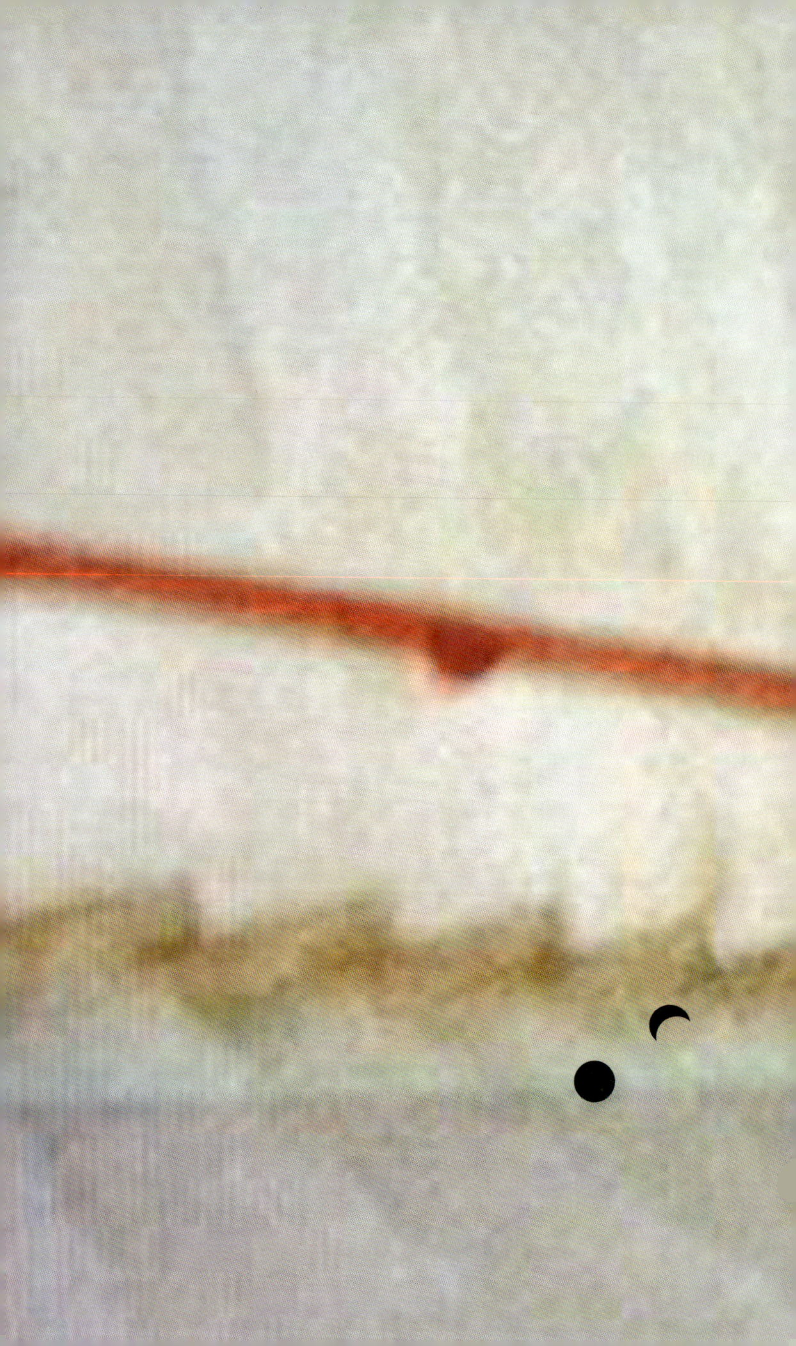

SOON AFTER

CHAPTER VII

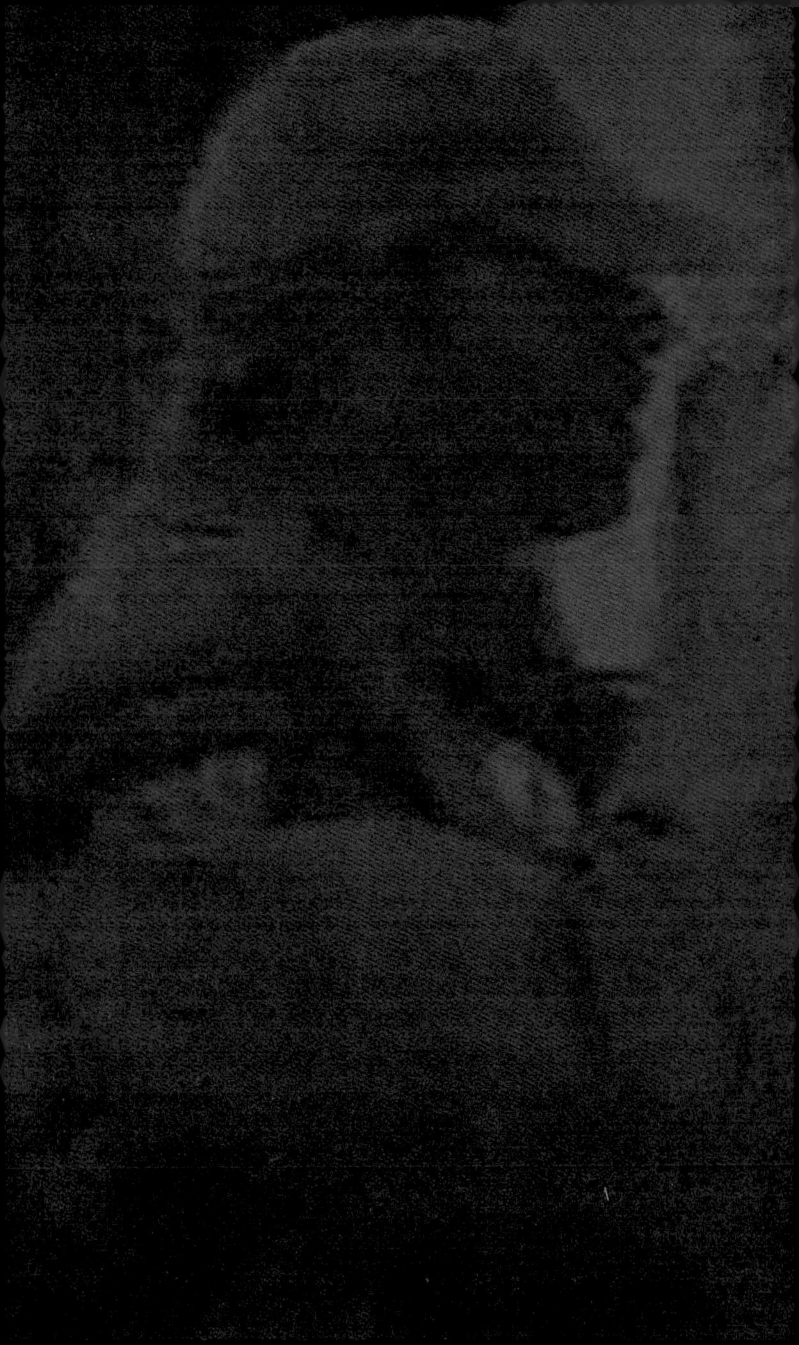

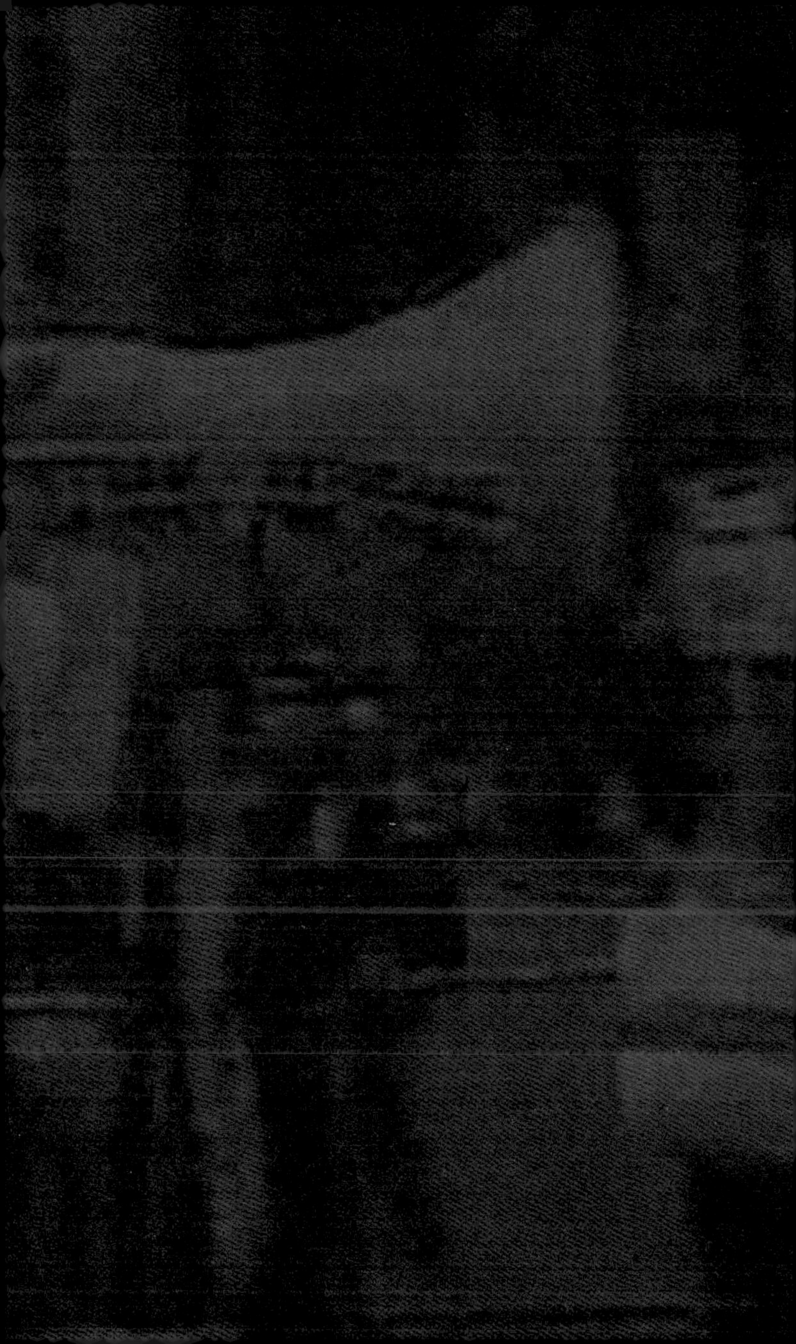

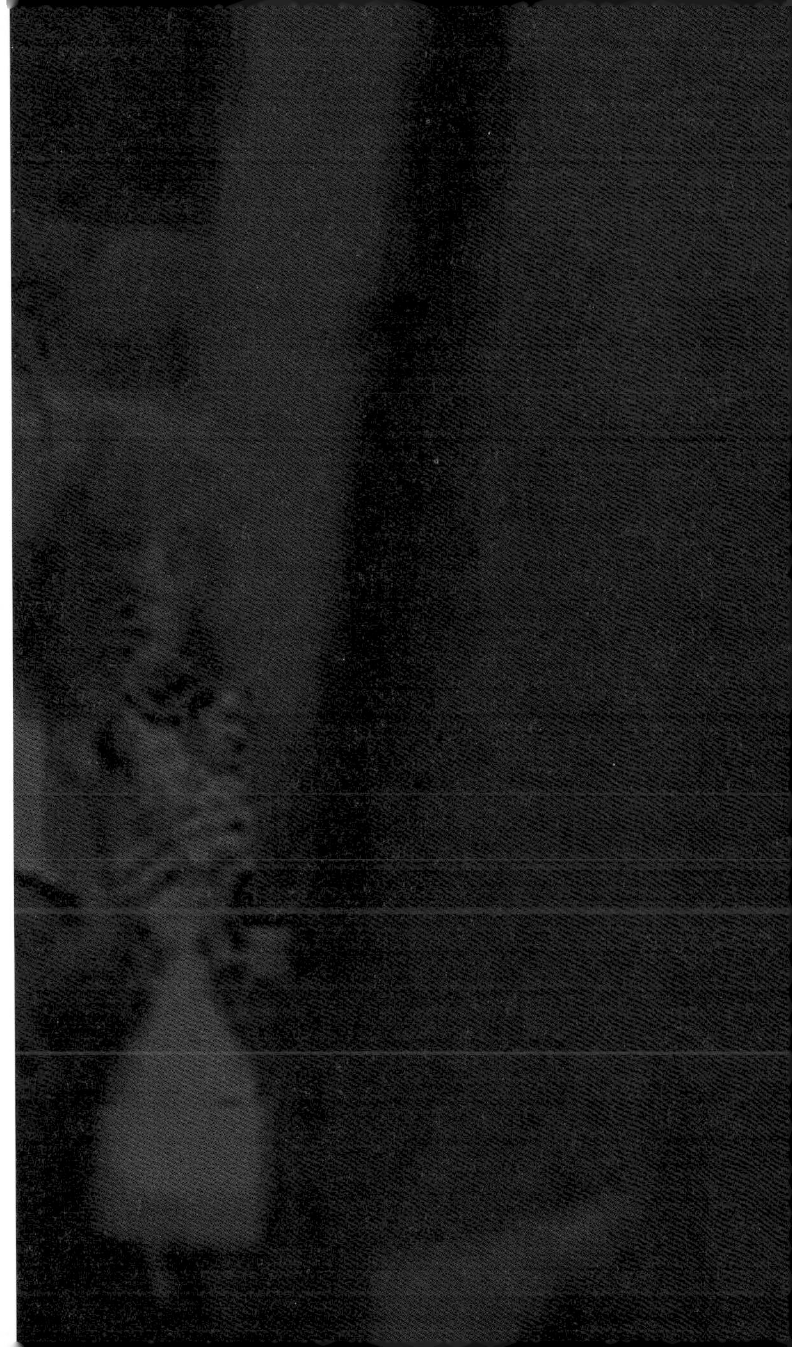

ONE

07.JPEG
09.JPEG
11.JPEG

08.JPEG
10.JPEG
12.JPEG

TROOP

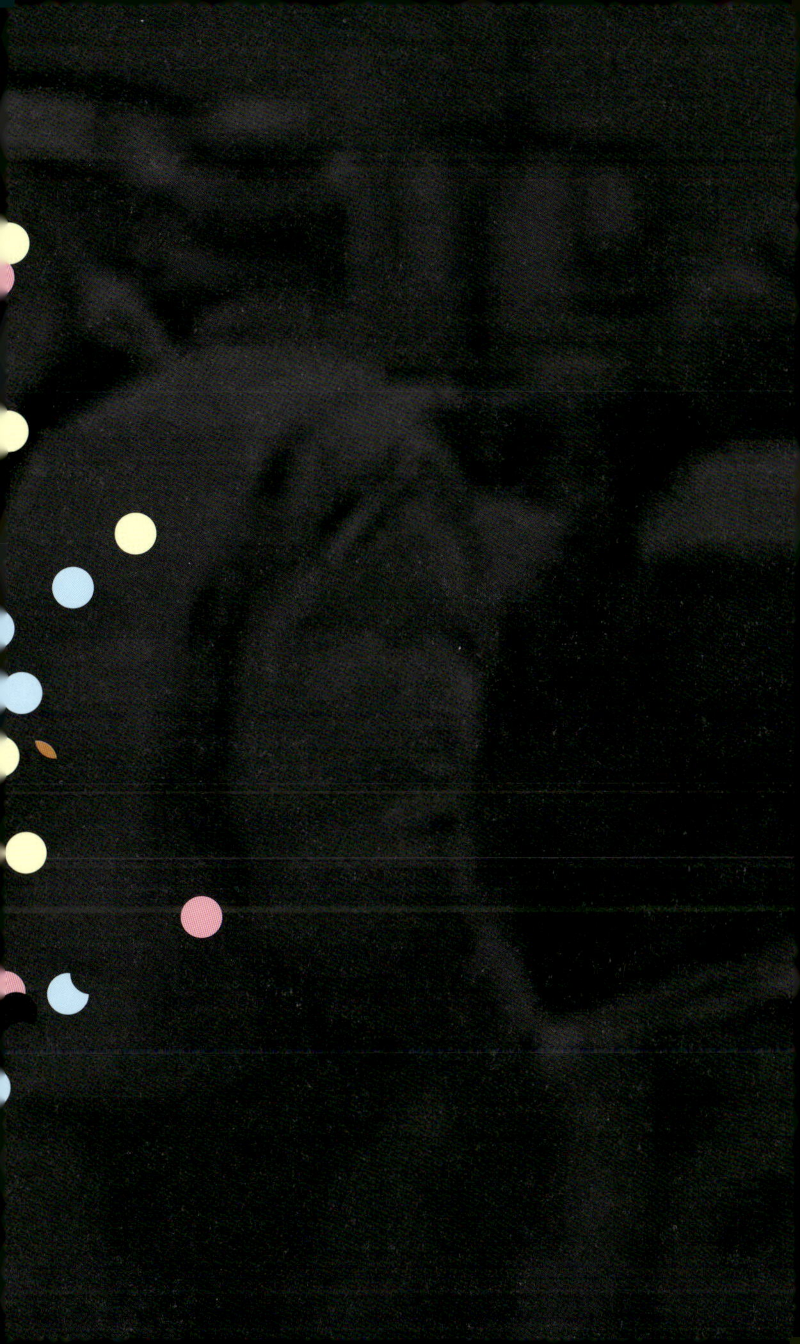

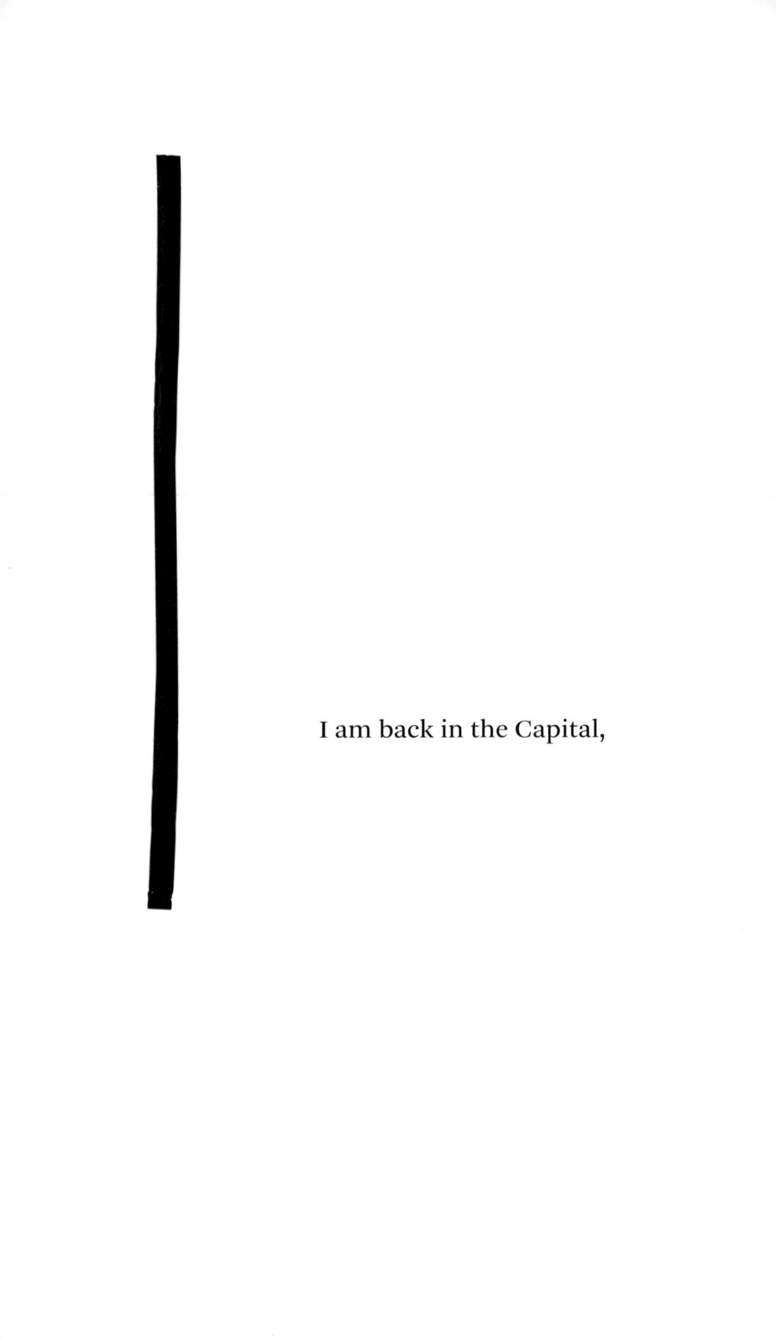

I am back in the Capital,

for the first time since the Events. There is a
march passing by in front of my hotel.

I watch it through the window of my room.
I check its live report on the muted flatscreen
while browsing through online news sites
on my laptop.

On TV, I notice a fraction-of-a-second delay
between the street version and its satellite
feed. The anchor says 'live report' but the
image keeps on lagging behind.

I feel prescient. I know what is going to happen even before it is aired.

I am done with television. I close my computer. I take my handbag, my cell phone, my electronic key card. I slip this book in the back pocket of my jeans.

I leave my room.
I take the elevator down.

Outside, in front of the building, I take a pause.
I watch the protesters as they pour along.
I wonder if...

>Slogans bounce back against the
>surrounding buildings.
>I catch the past of a slogan about
>the future, our future,

>after Empire.

Then, all of a sudden,
I decide to join the crowd.

There I am, marching.

Marching against the war.

I never thought I would ever do something
so retro. I feel awkward. Alone.
People must notice. They all came with
friends, relatives, like-minded colleagues.

I think about pretending to belong
to a group, any group. But I can't decide on
a single clique. There are simply too many.

I see labour militants, moderate

greens, vegan radicals, NGO subscribers.
A contingent of anarchists, grassroots
activists of all sorts. College students.
Blended households, men and women in
their eighties, toddlers and their pet dogs.

> They move as one.
> Or so it seems when framed
> through a camera lens.

I try a different pose, a more familiar one
this time: I pretend to have an incoming
call on my cell. While listening to no signal,
I look into several strangers' eyes. They
seem part of an indecisive sidewalk crowd.
They're there and they're not there. They
march and they don't march. Still in doubt
over the use of public protest.

> The exact same sense of futility
> washes over me.
> > I close my phone and

start moving.

Later he would write: *On the Fifteenth* February Day of the Year Three of the New Time, the Movement was back.

Later he would write: *In more than 600 cities* throughout the Empire, millions of people protested against the unilateral decision by the Federation to engage in a pre-emptive war against the Desert.

Later he would write: *The Imperial consensus* that had grown immediately after the Events had been replaced by important disagreements within the Imperial apparatus.

Later he would write: *Now, it is* the Empire that is divided, not the Multitude.
The Multitude is one.

We are the Multitude.
We hold the power.
We *are* power.

We sincerely believe that we can preempt
this preemptive war.
This war is not supposed to begin.
Our belief in our strength is unshakable.
We believe we will overcome.
We are so confident we don't even sing
the famous song.

　　We march.

　　I march.
　　For want of something else.

Loud posters in various languages. Sound
systems blare. Waves of singing, chanting
and drumming. Breakbeats expand across
the downtown area. A carnival atmosphere
pervades the big crowd. All are determined
to stay long after the helicopters finish
their count.

A continent away, some part-time imagery
analyst readjusts the gigapixel satellite cam
to focus on a group of young demonstrators
with kaffiyeh-covered faces.

The sun is low. It is almost the end of winter.

I have never seen so many people in one

place. Except for on television.
            It feels like it is 68 again.
            In 68 I was two.

            This is my march.
            This is our march.

    This is the march of our life.
            Our march is a parade.
                    A peace parade.
                    A love parade.
                    A life parade.

Marching I meet everybody I know.
Everybody I love. Everybody I want to know.
Everybody I want to love. Everybody I only
know from television. Everybody I love to
know only from television.

There are actors and actresses. There are
politicians and philosophers. There are
artists and musicians. There is this famous
writer too.

People recognize him. People
smile. People wave. People whisper
that he's severely ill. That he
wants to be there.

One more time.

To be one more time where history is
happening.

It is happening and I am there and it is
really happening and I'm still there.

This Saturday, history happened.
History happened and we forgot about it...

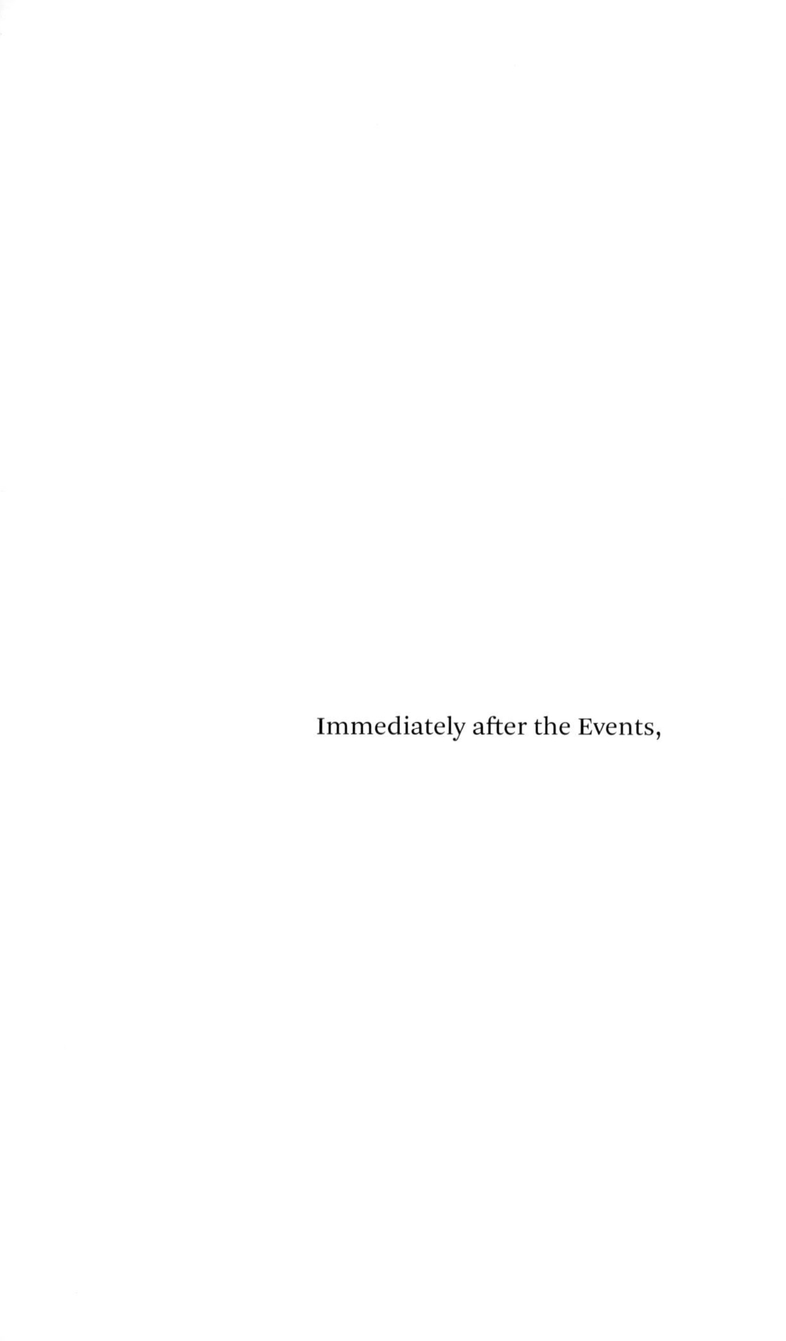

Immediately after the Events,

one persistent rumor had it that other hijacked
   planes were heading for the Studios.

        I remember.

        The thrill of it.

        The disappointment, too,
        that it turned out
        not to be true.

The Events are a terrible blow against
the Empire, he said. They destabilize the
Empire far more than they destabilize
the Federation.

> *Are you saying* that the Federation
> is no longer an Empire?, I asked.

The Federation has become part of the
Empire, he said. Although it likes to think
of itself as being the sole monarch, the
Federation is no longer an Empire in itself.
Empire is not founded on national sover-
eignty. The nation-state remains important.

> *Some more than* others, I added.

The power of Empire implies nation-states,
but it extends far beyond their prerogatives.
Empire is defined by a constant global
collaboration between monarchic, aristocratic
and democratic forces. Imperial sovereignty
is founded on this mixed constitution.

> *What about* Imperialism?, I asked.
> What about the long-standing
> mission of the Federation in
> its Peripheries?

Imperialism is over, he said. The Peripheries
have entered the centre. The glorious days

of the Federation are gone. These are Imperial
times. These are the times of the Empire.
He said.

And what if the Federation
is planning a coup d'état?,
I asked myself.

I saw everything. Everything.

Time and again.

Balls of fire against the Indian Summer sky.
'Oh my God!' a hundred times over. And
more, as a landmark high-rise collapses in
just under 15 seconds and some frames.

A cloud of smoke in pursuit of running
crowds on the bridge. These commuting
workers look round as if to freeze in their
mind the image of a skyline that is about
to disappear before their very eyes.

The last view of the Towers.
		I saw it. I'm sure I did.

I touch the 24 inch TV-screen for proof.

I am in the Confederacy. I am in the Capital.
I am in a senior staff meeting with a
member of the Confederate Commission.

We discuss tax regulations. For five minutes
or so we seriously consider the idea of Imperial
tax laws until a colleague Confederate
premium advisor bursts into laughter
and we all laugh along.
Then an outside world liaison
secretary comes in and tells us

about the unfolding Events.

It is half past three in the afternoon of the
Central Confederate Time Zone.
I immediately go looking for a television set
in the building where we have our meeting.

When I finally find a TV, I also find
a dozen office workers staring at it,
jaw-dropped, speechless.
         I leave the building. I instinctively
         take off my badge: it betrays that
         I am a member of a Federal
         delegation to the Confederacy.

I think of colleagues who walk around all
day and night in the Capital with their
badges bouncing on their belly, flaunting
their privilege. All they are allowed to do is to
enter a building in order to go to work.

I ask people in the street where
I can buy videotapes. I buy a dozen in a
Subcontinental night shop that happens
to be open during daytime too.
In my seven stars hotel room, I press the
record button on the VCR player. Convincing
myself that this makes sense. Knowing that
I won't be able to play those tapes back
home on my NTSC player.

I try to make a call to a friend

who's living on Great Jones Street.

I am not able to
reach him.

Everybody tries to call somebody.

Nobody is able
to reach anybody.

I keep an eye on television
                    all night long.

I surf the net incessantly. I wind up comfort
chatting with a rescue worker dazed from
staring into flood lights at the disaster scene.

I drink everything from the minibar. I don't care much for the Breaking News footage of cheering Territorialists.

Either those images are faked, or they have been shot previously to the Events, on some other Occasion.

There is also this rumour about five people from the Zone arrested in the Submetropolis after witness reports to the police about cheering at the view of the collapsing Towers, filming, high-fiving.
I don't believe these rumours about Zoniacs either.

Sure, there are some maniacs in the Zone, just as there are some terrorists in the Territories.

That doesn't mean all Territorialists are Terrorists. Neither are all Zoniacs maniacs.

They built the Wall. The Zoniacs built this insane Wall. The Wall is built in order to be able to celebrate unity after the Wall has been hated, slammed, drilled, demolished and destroyed.

I remember before the Wall.
Before the Checkpoints. Before the
Passports. So many years ago. Seems like
another age. The dead are still there. You
just have to look at the old TV broadcasts
instead of the new blog reports. Too many
settlements. Nothing has been settled. The
Conflict has become routine. Watching the
Conflict has become routine. It is as ugly as
it ever was.

Still, things are
different now.

This side of the Wall people keep a record
of what is happening in their everyday lives.
Permitting perfect strangers to monitor and
comment their every move and thought.

Login link edit create submit tag reply.

Growing numbers of users view each other's
low-res images. Trained spectators skilled
in answering visuals with visuals.

Sign in splice swap tag share stream.

Historians would refer to today
as the Postwar period.
For some.

For others,

the war never stopped. It just took on a
different form: numerous incursions, night
raids, targeted killings, demolition of
houses, the uprooting of farmland, the
building of a Wall.
  A matter of safety, they say.
  A matter of security.

The Wall is a line of defence against a looming
army of martyrs. A desperate move to prevent
them from blowing up citizens at a rush
hour bus terminal. From blowing themselves
up at a crowded wifi hot-spot.

This is the ultimate message the martyrs
are sending us:
  your body does not belong to you.

  Your body belongs
  to the Empire.

  Like money belongs to the Treasury.

Blowing yourself up is as scandalous as
burning cash money.

Sooner or later, Zoniacs and Territorialists
are going to tear down that Wall and share

the same Land.
The time has come to give up on staring
death in the eye. To give up on the desperation
some kids learn to call martyrdom. To finally
and definitively give up on the warrior code.

The time has come to think
the unthinkable. To create a new flag.

Homeland is a failed idea.

One Land for
two peoples.

One Land for
many peoples.

To dream of a nation.

'Vouloir penser la révolution serait
l'équivalent au réveil de vouloir
la logique dans l'incohérence des
images rêvées.' 'Trying to think
the revolution is like waking up
and trying to see the logic in a
dream.' Jean Genet.

He was enchanted by the fedayeen. Took their
side. Lived among them. Still, the day they
would have become a nation like any other
nation, he would no longer have been there.

To dream of a nation.

When the nation
does not yet
            exist.

When the nation
remains merely
          a dream.

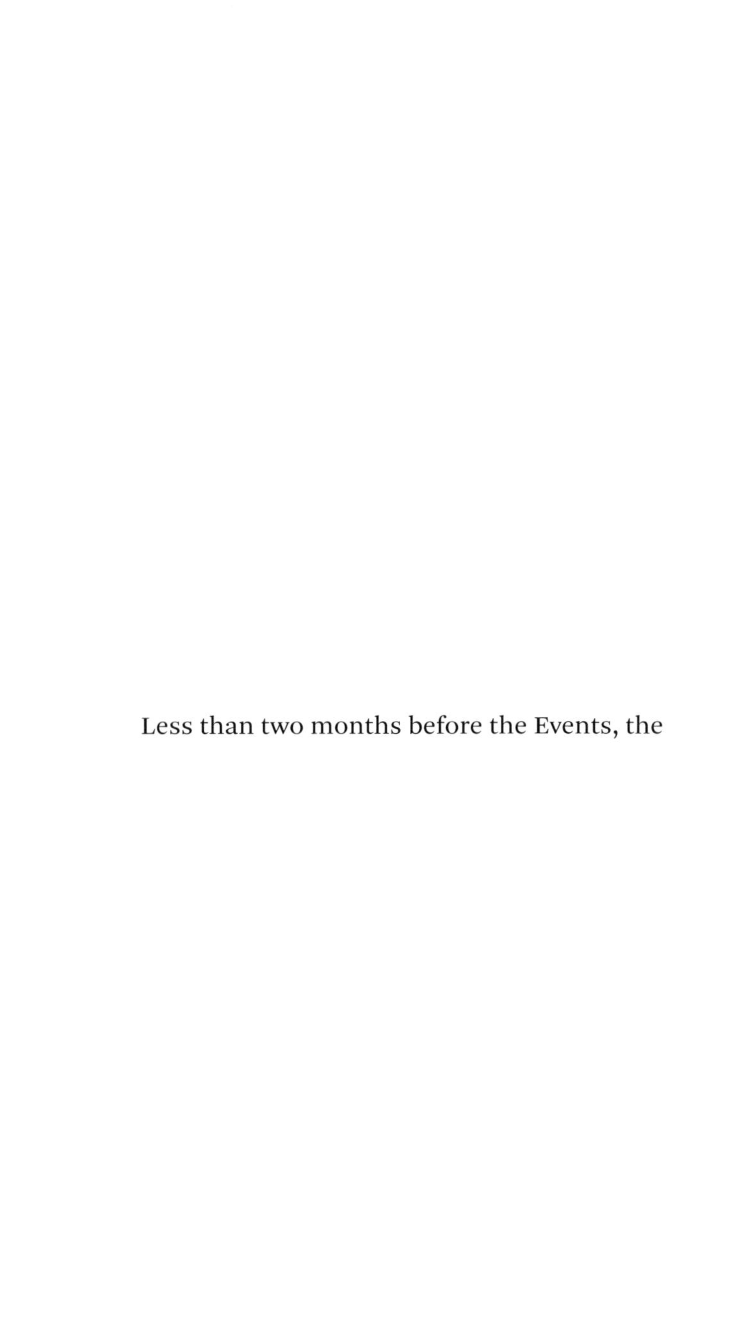

Less than two months before the Events, the

Movement held a huge celebration in the Port.
  Never before so many people from so many
  different backgrounds had protested
  against the Empire.

  I remember the Empire being terribly
  scared by this growing non-violent protest
  of the Multitude.
            One would think it was
            just another march.

  Yet the airspace above the Port was closed.

The Portuarian army had put up anti-aircraft missiles. The President of the Federation was residing offshore.

Secret Services somehow seemed aware of terror tactics to come: hijacked passenger planes used as missiles against highly symbolic Federal targets.
At first, the Movement considered Empire's military bravado as the usual but somewhat exaggerated display of power.

Until it became clear that the Red Zone in the centre of the Port had been declared off-limits and surrounded by a barricade, leaving protesters no opportunity to communicate with Empire delegates. They saw the padded jackets, the riot clubs, the helmets and the bandanas concealing the policemen's faces.

They started singing
'stiamo arrivando, bastardi st
to the tune of 'Guantanamera'.

They were beaten, kicked, taken into custody. Dozens hospitalized.
One shot dead.

A celebration of dissent mobilized by waves
of text messages commemorated by the video
evidence of a body lying in a pool of red.
His blood flows like the river, like time.

I saw it.
I'm sure I did.
First on the evening news. Then on the
front page of the morning paper. And
later, repeatedly on tribute sites to the
fallen fighter.

I saw everything.
Still, I'd not be able to summon his name in
tonight's quiz show.

o arrivando'

Mid-summer wears on
as if nothing has happened.

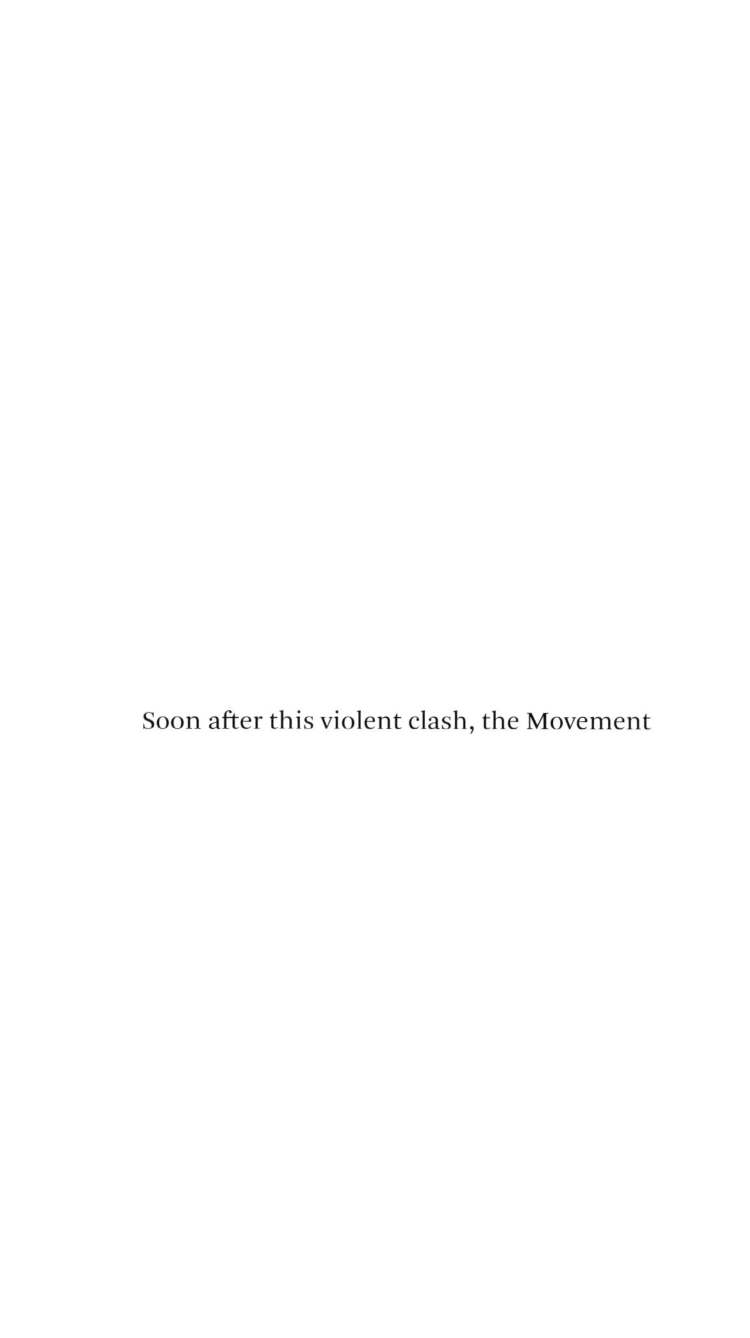
Soon after this violent clash, the Movement

immediately started to prepare for even
   bigger manifestations in the Federal
   Capital. But a few weeks later, as a
   consequence of the Events, the annual
   meeting of the Imperial Fund and the
   Imperial Bank were cancelled. And so, the
   planned protests of the Movement were
   cancelled too.

> After the Events, all protest,
> even if it was peaceful,
> was frowned upon.

It seemed inappropriate to annoy the
Imperial leaders with social, economic
and ecological complaints, now that they
had more important things on their minds.

Whenever a manifestation took a grim turn,
there would be the stigma of vandalism,
rioting, terrorism, absolute evil.

After the Events, the Empire professed an
oecumenism of peace.

I remember Imperial plane traffic totally
disrupted and my return flight cancelled.

>   I am stuck
>   in the Capital.

I wind up on the square in front of the stock
exchange. On this busiest of crossroads in
the centre of the city, no Confederate citizen
moves.
>   For want of something else.

On the busiest crossroad in the centre of
every city, no Confederate citizen speaks.

>   For want of something else.

Entire cities rise up in silence.

For three
long minutes.

For three long minutes, it felt as if we were

one people, one world.

                              A silence echoing
                around the globe.

I forgot all about it until weeks later the air strikes started and I was watching the electric green night scenes on cable TV. My dog especially took to the inaudible loudness of the bombs-eye views.

Later he would write: *Paradoxically, the* Empire was strengthened by the blow that hit the Federation.

Later he would write: *Due to the* Events, Imperial consensus got this very specific meaning: our way of life was endangered by terror. The Events were interpreted not as a strike against 'the Federation's way of life' but as an attack on the post-historic democracy of all Imperial human beings.

Later he would write: *Despotic regimes were* tied in even more strongly into the multilayered structure of the Empire: one didn't ask that they would become democratic. It was sufficient that they would strongly condemn the attacks and that they would cooperate in the Imperial war on terror.

As the Empire left these despotic regions undisturbed in exchange for its Governors to support the war against terror, it gave the people who hated the Governors for their despotism even more reasons for their terror against the Empire.

After the Events, the Movement continued its manifestations, but its momentum seemed lost. The Multitude that had protested against the Imperial Meeting in the Port was now disrupted, broken. It needed to reinvent itself, to reflect on new tactics and strategies.

Until word came that the Federation would storm the Desert. For the King of the Desert was hiding a frightening Plan. While everybody knew that the King of the Desert had no Plan whatsoever.

I remember the announcement of the Operation. Heads of State lying on camera. Mainstream media in on the con game. I was with Confederate friends, they all looked at me as if it had been my personal idea. I felt terribly ashamed to have a Federal passport.

The Movement reconstituted itself, it took form and shape anew in protests and actions throughout the Empire. Its resistance affected parts of the Empire itself. Important regions, such as the Tundra and the Steppe regions, eternal members of the Imperial Security Board, made ample reservations and some threatened to use their veto against a military action by the Federation and its Allies.

ending this. Two people embrace as the

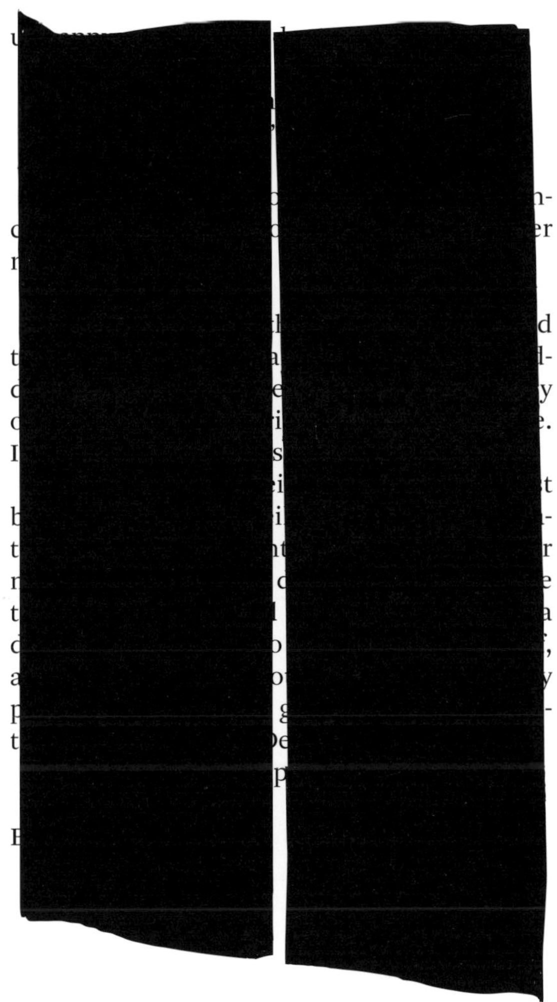

The Bund too, an economic power and coincidentally in that period non-eternal member of the Imperial Security Board, heavily resisted a military campaign in the Desert.

I remember my enthusiasm when I heard the minister of Imperial Affairs of the Bund address the startled Federal premium secretary of Defence at an Imperial Security Conference. I even tried to memorise the Post-historic words the minister spoke.

'*Wir verdanken die* Federation unsere Demokratie, die Federation ist unverzichtbar für Frieden und Stabilität. Aber für den Bund hat sie eine ganz besondere Bedeutung. Weil wir uns nicht selbst befreit haben, und weil wir unsere Demokratie ohne ihre Hilfe nicht aufgebaut hätten. Nur meine Generation hat dabei gelernt: You have to make the case, and to make the case in a democracy, you have to be convinced yourself, and excuse me, I am not convinced. This is my problem and I cannot go to the people of the Bund and say, 'well, let's go to war because there are reasons and so on,' and I don't believe in that'.

I was moved to tears when I heard the brave
man speak. Television does that to me.

A president delivers his inaugural address. A
sprinter sets the world 100 metres record. An
8-year old kid performs a cover in some junior
talent show. Two people embrace as the happy
ending unfolds. Two people embrace as the
unhappy ending unfolds.

And I cry.

'You have to make the case.'

'I am not convinced.'

Imperial reason is calling
the Federation to Imperial order.

And I cry.

That Friday the sun was shining. Late in the afternoon it had rained. Then the rain had stopped. We were sitting in a fancy bar, sipping at our Twin Fizz.

Most of the regulars were exfeds, Federal citizens with a mission in the Capital of the Confederacy.

We were all waiting for something to happen. And we didn't like what was likely to happen.

Almost everyone in the room was texting. Responding incoming messages by forwarding them. Telecom companies must have seen their sms revenues double in no time.

You didn't like these places full of 'badges', as you labeled these exfeds. And although I was one of them too, I didn't wear a badge. You thought that was a very smart thing to do.

The military power of the Federation is troubling the Empire, you whispered. As if you were telling me a military secret. As if you were encouraging me to use this information in a secret briefing.

The Events have been a humiliating experience for the Federation. It became obsessed with proving its strength. And now it comes up with crazy plans that are all completely counterproductive. Like in old stories, the Federation is like a king going mad, while princes and dukes and bishops were thinking of what to do with a mad king.

I nodded.

And you guys, you said, as you raised your glass to some of the badges at the bar, you Federal guys are the princes and dukes and bishops of this tale. It seems there is very little you can do, except wait and hope that things will happen. And get another drink!

They laughed as loud as they could and did as you told them they should. It was time to get my coat and return to my hotel that was also yours.

And then things happened.

I know what that sounds like.

But that's not what I mean.

Even though these things may
have happened too.

We were both drunk. I was confused. You were
impressed. The usual excuses. But then again,
that's is not what I mean.

What happened was that
the Movement rebooted.

The Movement that seemed to have crashed
shortly after the Events,
this Movement, restarted.

Much to the distress of my many colleague
premium advisors of the Federation, the Movement wanted the Federation to reconsider.
They thought they had think-tanked everything over. They thought they had a premium
plan. They thought they had everything checked
and double-checked. They thought they could
get away with it. They were so confident.

But the Movement didn't buy it.

And while it criticized the Federation, it
praised the Confederacy for being thoughtful
and wise. Federal advisors used to think of their
Confederate colleagues as their little siblings,
whom they had to learn everything.

They thought it unlikely that the Confederacy would become the Imperial leader of the New Time.

And for sure they
didn't wish that to happen.

It seemed however that this was exactly what the Movement called for: a dramatic shift in Imperial leadership from Federation to Confederacy.

The next day, the newspaper headline read: 'Clash between two superpowers – the Federation versus worldwide public opinion'.

But it wasn't about the Federation. It was about the Empire. The Movement didn't want to bring down the Empire. Instead, it pushed for a rearticulation of its structure.

The Movement was heading towards a stand-off with Empire.

This Saturday, history happened.
One more time.

When I wake up, I hear voices on the streets. I notice you have left the room. I put on my jeans, my bra, my shirt. I take my handbag, my mobile phone, my electronic key card.

As I want to leave the room, this book slips from my back pocket, falls on the plush carpet floor. I pick it up. I put in in my handbag.
A black brick.

I leave my room. I take the elevator down. Outside, in front of the building, I take a pause.
I watch the people as they pour by.
I wonder if...

Slogans bounce back against the surrounding buildings. I catch the past of a slogan about the future, our future, after Empire. Then, all of a sudden, a phosphorescent flare rises over the crowd. The cold breeze of the present. I look up. I see myself looking up. As if history already ran its course. Intense white flashes tingled with orange fill the screen. A serious fuzz in the soundtrack. Tonight, investigative news magazines will be displaying military maps and 3-D animation targets.

A week from now, I will watch a panoramic view of dark smoke ascending above a cityscape

where disaster has struck early in the evening.
There is no crime in watching. Is there?

This is the march of our life.
The ephemeral world of connectivity.

A peace parade.
Act now as if the future you want
to bring about is already here.

A life parade.
Because words are actions and
they make things happen.

On the Fifteenth February Day
of the Year Three of the New Time,
the Movement was back.

October never comes.

I decide to join the crowd.
        For want of something else.

AUGUSTE ORTS

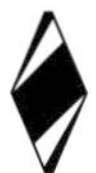

LUCA
CAMPUS
SINT-LUKAS
BRUSSEL

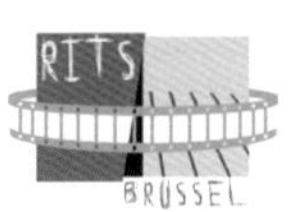

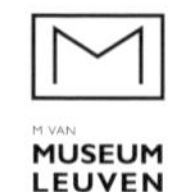

published by AraMER, an imprint of MER.
Paper Kunsthalle, Geldmunt 36, 9000 Gent,
Belgium · www.merpaperkunsthalle.org
distributed by Exhibitions International,
Kol. Begaultlaan 17, 3012 Leuven, Belgium
www.exhibitionsinternational.org
executive production by Auguste Orts,
Brussels, Belgium · www.augusteorts.be
design by Maaike & Fairuz · www. garage64.be
with the support of LUCA Campus Sint-Lukas
Brussels, RITS School of Arts (Erasmus
University College Brussels), M Museum
Leuven, Square Brussels.
thanks to Pieter Van Bogaert, Marie Logie,
Jan Cools, Eva Wittocx, Ann Clicteur,
Ina Wudtke, Agna Smisdom & Kobe.

ISBN 978 94 9069 394 7
D/2013/7852/158

This book is published at the occasion of
Blijven Kijken / Ce qui nous regarde / Dropouts
at M Museum Leuven, 14 02 13 – 12 05 13.
A group show curated by Pieter Van Bogaert,
including Herman Asselberghs' 2010 video
piece *After Empire.*

15 FEB. 2003